ERNEST NYS

THE PAPACY
CONSIDERED IN RELATION TO
INTERNATIONAL LAW

Elibron Classics
www.elibron.com

Elibron Classics series.

ISBN 0-543-97812-5 (paperback)
ISBN 0-543-97811-7 (hardcover)

This Elibron Classics Replica Edition is an unabridged facsimile of the edition published in 1879 by Henry Sweet, London.

The Papacy

Translated from the French

THE PAPACY

CONSIDERED IN RELATION TO

INTERNATIONAL LAW.

BY

ERNEST NYS,
DOCTEUR EN DROIT.

Translated from the French

BY THE REV. PONSONBY A. LYONS,
Editor of "Whitaker's History of Whalley."

LONDON:
HENRY SWEET, 3, CHANCERY LANE,
Law Publisher.
1879.

TO

THE RIGHT HONORABLE

SIR ROBERT PHILLIMORE, D.C.L.,

MEMBER OF HER MAJESTY'S MOST HONORABLE PRIVY COUNCIL

AND JUDGE OF THE HIGH COURT OF ADMIRALTY,

THIS ESSAY

IS

RESPECTFULLY INSCRIBED

By the AUTHOR.

The Papacy

AND

INTERNATIONAL LAW.

One of the most interesting problems of international law is that of the international position of the Papacy in our time. Eight years ago, the sovereign pontiffs found themselves deprived of the temporal power which they had exercised for centuries; and of the double character with which they had been invested, there now remains to them merely that of supreme chiefs of the Roman Catholic Church. As long as Rome was subject to them, they had, like all sovereigns, a juridical international personality; they enjoyed the rights conferred by this personality, and were subject to the obligations it implies. The events of 1870, the entry of the Italian troops into the Eternal City, the suppression of the Roman States, would appear necessarily to induce great changes, and to have modified the status of the Holy See.

It might at first have been supposed that Europe would regulate the new condition of the Holy See. Projects of this kind were attributed to the empire of Germany. But no resolution was taken. Some states profited by the march of events to withdraw their representatives from Rome. Others maintained the *status quo*. After 1870, Pius IX. had his nuncios as he had before; after, as before, he saw powers accredit their ambassadors to his person. Even his death has not as yet modified this state of things, and Leo XIII. has, like his predecessors, been able to notify to the different governments his accession to the pontifical throne; like them, he maintains diplomatic relations, and, at this moment, negotiations are going on, with a view of renewing with several countries the relations which the policy of Pius IX. had broken off (*a*).

From a theoretical point of view, there is here a flagrant anomaly. The only persons known to international law are States (*b*). Outside of them, nothing is capable of rights or subject to duties. Primitive or absolute rights, conditional or hypothetical rights, rights arising from pacific or hostile relations, are, like the duties corresponding to these rights, the exclusive attribute of sovereignty. Now, there is no sovereignty except in the State. As soon, then, as the temporal power of the popes fell, their international status would vanish. They would not, and could not, have international rights or duties.

The facts, however, are far from being in conformity with principles. In the past, the sovereign pontiffs have already been seen to send out, as popes, not as kings, their legates and nuncios, and to negotiate Concordats not relating either to the Patrimony of St. Peter, or to the interests of their subjects (*c*). Eight years have elapsed since the fall of the temporal power. We have stated what was done for Pius IX.; we have told what is now done for Leo XIII. One of the principal rights of sovereignty—the right of legation and treaty—has been exercised, and is still exercised.

Where is the error? Is it in the theory or in the practice? Has or has not the Papacy an international status? Constituted as it is, a supposed spiritual power,

(*a*) The States still actually represented at the Vatican are:—Austria and Hungary, Spain, France, and Portugal, who have each an ambassador at Rome; Bavaria, Belgium, Bolivia, Brazil, Ecuador, Chili, Guatemala, Monaco, the Republic of Nicaragua, Peru, and the Republic of San Salvador, who maintain a minister plenipotentiary. Germany has retained a chancellor. Holland has no minister accredited to the Holy See, but an internuncio continues to reside at the Hague.

(*b*) Bluntschli, *Das Völkerrecht der civilisirten Staten*, Book II. art. 16 et seq.

(*c*) Bluntschli, *De la responsabilité et de l'irresponsabilité du Pape dans le droit international.* Translated from the German by A. Rivier.

deprived of all real and effective sovereignty, can it enjoy a primordial prerogative of sovereign States? This is the problem which we find placed before us.

The question assuredly deserves to be examined. Few institutions have played a part in the world comparable to that of the Papacy. For centuries the annals of the Holy See have been confounded with those of Catholicism itself. It was the bishops of Rome who created, so to say, the Catholic Church; it was they who gave it its formidable organization; and it was they who impressed upon it that impulse which long made it the arbiter of the destinies of humanity. On this account alone the study of their international rights and duties presents great interest. But the Papacy has not a merely historical character. Now, as in the Middle Ages, the sovereign pontiffs find themselves at the head of Catholicism. Theoretically, the popes of the nineteenth century are even more supreme than their predecessors; and what in Gregory VII., Innocent III., and Boniface VIII. was simply an affirmation of haughty pretensions, has become for Roman Catholics a dogma of faith with respect to Pius IX. and his successors. The Constitution *Pastor Æternus* of 18th July, 1870, has this bearing, that henceforth, literally, the Pope is the Church. And whatever may be the feeling entertained on the subject of Catholicism,—whatever may be the opinion held as to its mission, and the manner in which that mission has been fulfilled,—it is impossible to ignore the influence which it yet in our days exercises on the march of civilization. It cannot, then, be superfluous to study the status of him who personifies it.

History, the *living word of law*, as one of the great minds of contemporary Germany so well calls it, will serve us as a guide in our labour. We will examine by its light the Roman theories on the subject which occupies us; we will study the attempts which have preceded, and the facts which have accompanied, the putting into practice of these theories, and we will try to educe what we believe to be sound ideas. The problem, however, is confined within sufficiently narrow limits. It cannot be required to examine if the Papacy possesses a complete and perfect sovereignty. A multitude of international rights cannot in any case be acknowledged to belong to it; and it will be finally sufficient to examine whether it is allowable to admit that the Papacy possesses a sovereignty *sui generis* which gives it the right of legation and treaty.

I.

The science of international law is modern. If, however, it had existed in antiquity, the situation of a pretended spiritual power could not have found a place among its objects. In reality the very idea of such a power did not exist. Religion was, above all, national; the political community included the spiritual, and the *jus sacrum* was merely a division of the *jus publicum*. To the pagan idea Jesus opposed the idea of the separation of the two domains,—spiritual and temporal; and by the side of the earthly kingdom, He proclaimed the heavenly kingdom into which all those might enter who acknowledged Him to be the Messiah, who followed His precepts, and laboured like Him to the glory of his Father (*d*). The new religion was born.

Was it intended by its Founder to assume a tangible form, and is the conception of an outward Church a conception truly Christian? Neander (*e*) has completely proved that the Church is a deviation from the Gospel spirit; that it constitutes a return to Judaism. Moses had organized a priesthood called on to offer sacrifices, to serve as intermediary between God and man. Jesus restored direct communion between the believer and his

(*d*) Geffcken, *Staat und Kirche in ihrem Verhältniss geschichtlich entwickelt*.

(*e*) Neander, *Geschichte der christlichen Religion*, Vol. I. pp. 306 et seq.

Creator. He alone is mediator; He alone is a sacrificer. Doubtless all Christians are not endowed with the same gifts; but he who is called on to teach the faith is not the superior of those to whom he preaches the divine word. External unity is an idea of the ancient law. Under the new law there exists a more true and a higher unity,—the unity of minds.

Christianity in its pure form may then exist without raising any question of international law. Jesus and the apostles did not cease to preach submission to temporal authority. The first Christians were satisfied with progressing and recruiting their numbers under the guardianship of the existing laws; and, on the other hand, the government of the Church was long in the hands of the faithful.

To this democratic organization the episcopal aristocracy succeeded (*f*). The bishops claimed a divine origin. But even in this larger sphere equality continued to exist. The idea of spiritual power had assumed a bodily form In turn episcopal aristocracy disappeared. Too weak to resist the social dissolution to which the world was a prey, it was replaced by the Papacy; and in this the power of the Church concentrated itself. On the ground of reason, the pretension set up by the Papacy of constituting a spiritual power was unfounded. Nevertheless it gained ground.

The bishops of Rome did not long consent to remain the equals of the bishops of other Christian communities. It is curious to see that even in the primitive Church Pope Victor declared the Christians of Asia Minor separated from his communion; and in the third century Pope Stephen claimed to impose on the Churches of Africa and Asia the Roman tradition as to the validity of baptism. The movement which took place towards the

(*f*) Laurent, *Etudes sur l'histoire de l'humanité*, Tome V., *Les Barbares et le Catholicisme*, pp. 274 et seq.

end of the second century, and the beginning of which is marked by the institution of provincial synods, must have favoured these pretensions of the popes. The synod was held in the principal town of the province, and the bishop of this town, *the metropolitan*, presided over it, and gained by this a certain *prestige*. The movement became more marked; the associations extended and embraced wider territories. It furnished a new motive for deference to some episcopal cities. Rome had been considered as the ecclesiastical metropolis of Italy. Soon she divided with Alexandria and Antioch the honour of being one of the three most important Sees of Christendom. The tradition of St. Peter's going to the capital of the empire found general credence; Rome was considered the only episcopal See founded in the West by an apostle; and the *primatus honoris* given to St. Peter was reflected on his pretended successors. The Council of Sardica (344) even sanctioned this pre-eminence by allowing the condemned bishops to appeal to Rome; and an edict of Valentinian III., in which the weakness of the ruler was hidden by pompous language, acknowledged the primacy of Leo the Great.

After the fall of the Roman Empire, the Ostrogoth princes, in general, allowed the western hierarchy a freedom of which the Churches of the East were deprived; and, while the emperors of Constantinople made the ecclesiastical laws exactly as they made the civil laws, contenting themselves with sending the first to the patriarchs as they addressed the latter to the prefects, Theodoric allowed a synod to declare illegal and inadmissible the interference of laics in spiritual affairs. No doubt equal tolerance was not always exhibited. John I. died in prison, and his successor Felix III. was imposed by the king on the choice of the Roman senate, clergy, and people. But neither these facts, nor yet the conquest of Italy by the Greek emperors, could prevent the ascending march of the papal institution.

The pretensions of the Papacy called forth numberless

protestations. The East has never admitted them; the patriarchs of Alexandria and Antioch refused to submit, the patriarch of Constantinople relied on the authority of the council of Chalcedon to prove that his rights were equal to those of Rome. But Rome held out. She had the genius of unity, and the East, torn by the spirit of division inherent in the Greek race, could not stop her.

With respect to the civil power, Rome still continued to occupy a subordinate position. Justinian united in his hands the spiritual and temporal power. He overwhelmed Rome with honours, yet did not the less maintain his own supremacy. He caused two of his creatures to be nominated popes, and the very humble letter of Gregory the Great to the Emperor Maurice, shows better than anything the respective situation of the Papacy and the Empire.

Notwithstanding the weakness of the imperial power in Italy, and the invasions of the Lombards, Rome continued dependant on the emperors of Constantinople; the sovereign pontiffs received from them, or from their representatives, the exarchs of Ravenna, confirmation of their election, and were subject to payment of taxes. Even the Carlovingians merely followed the Byzantine tradition. Though they liberated the popes from the rule of the Lombards and the Greeks, they placed them in the same rank as the other bishops of their vast empire, and the formula of the oath which the popes had to take before obtaining their confirmation, the letters of many of them, the conduct of Leo III. in justifying himself by oath before Charlemagne, and that of Pascal in defending himself before the envoys of Louis le Débonnaire, all testify to the subordinate position in political affairs occupied by the popes, who for a century had proudly assumed the title of universal bishop.

The fact of temporal sovereignty, of which Sutri, acquired in 728, was the nucleus, did not introduce at the beginning much change in their international situation. The popes obtained successively the Byzantine cities Amelia, Orta, Bomarzo, and Bieda; Pepin le Bref even made the sovereign pontiff Patrician of the Exarchat; and the weakness of the successors of Charlemagne seemed to assure the independence of the See of Rome. But a period of debasement, crime and vice soon menaced the Papacy with an irremediable downfall. Sergius III., John X., John XII., Benedict IX., Sylvester III., were slaves to the vilest passions, and the intervention of the kings of Germany was required to save the Catholic Church. Otho I., king of Germany, deposed John XII. (963), and appointed Leo VIII. in his place. The constitution of this last is remarkable. Its authenticity has certainly been contested by Baronius, but Gieseler has defended it successfully. "Largimur domno Ottoni . . . . ejusque successoribus hujus regni Italiæ in perpetuum facultatem eligendi successorem, atque summæ Sedis Apostolicæ Pontificem ordinandi: ac per hoc archiepiscopos seu episcopos, ut ipsi ab eo investituram accipiant, et consecrationem unde debent, exceptis his quos Imperator pontificibus et archiepiscopis concessit" (*g*). The scandal came to an end. At the synod of Sutri (1046), Henry III. deposed three rival popes, and raised a German, the bishop of Bamberg, to the supreme dignity.

The Papacy had incurred another peril. The national Churches had shown themselves jealous of their independence; the English Episcopate and the Gallican Church had refused to recognize the authority of Rome, even in matters of dogma. The danger was averted. But in the eleventh century it seemed as if the Papacy would be, this time, for ever vanquished in the struggle it had undertaken to assure its domination. It was to be saved by the genius of one man.

When only a monk, Hildebrand had inspired the Holy

(*g*) O. Mejer, *Institutionen des gemeinen deutschen Kirchenrechtes*, § 13; Gieseler, *Kirchengeschichte*, Vol. II. Part I. § 22.

See. He had been the counsellor of Leo IX., Victor II., Stephen IX., Nicholas II., and had urged them successively to labour at the regeneration of the Church, and to assure to the Papacy the spiritual power. When Pope, he continued this gigantic enterprise (*h*).

Two vices infected Christianity—simony, and the immorality of the clergy. It was these vices that Gregory VII., during his whole life, assailed with a vigour, a persistance, a grandeur, in both conception and action, such as the world had not yet witnessed. His predecessors had struggled against the episcopate; he strove against the entire clergy. This part of his work was crowned with success. The unity of the Church was assured, and his spiritual power was acknowledged. But the idea of a spiritual power belonging to the Church implied domination over the temporal power. Hence new struggles, and hence the arrogant and even startling theories of the Papacy in the middle ages—theories which aimed at nothing less than establishing the most absolute Theocracy.

The terrible wars which Gregory VII. waged against the Empire are well known. He did not affirm in Germany alone the supreme authority of the Church and its head. He wrote to his legates in France that it was necessary "to enjoin on all the French, and order them by true obedience, to pay at least one penny a year for each house." "Your kingdom is a property of St. Peter's," he said to the Princes of Spain. "Take the oath of a vassal," he wrote to William the Conqueror. He used similar language to the Corsicans, the Sardinians, and the Hungarians. But it is in his struggle against Henry IV. of Germany that we see him exhibit the greatest audacity. The war in which the scene of Canossa is one of the most memorable episodes, was in truth a war for the empire of the world. It broke out on the occasion of simony. Henry IV. had just ascended the throne. He

(*h*) Laurent, *Etudes sur l'histoire de l'humanité*, Tome V., *La Papauté et l'Empire.*

refused to submit to the requirements of Rome. The Pope, certain of finding strong support among the Princes of the Empire, did not hesitate to summon him before the Council. Germany protested, and her bishops replied to the challenge of the Pope by deposing Gregory himself at the Council of Worms. The Pope excommunicated the Emperor, and absolved his subjects from their oath of obedience. "I forbid Henry," said the Papal bull, "to govern the Teutonic kingdom and Italy, I absolve all Christians from the oath they have taken to him or may take, and I forbid all to serve him as king."

The strife was formidable. It had alternatives of success and defeat. Vanquished for once, the Emperor went to implore at Canossa the clemency of Gregory VII. (*i*); but soon he took up arms again and remained indomitable. Neither sixty-five battles, nor calumny, nor

(*i*) Gregory VII. has preserved for us an account of the scene of Canossa. In a letter addressed to the subjects of Henry IV. he expresses himself as follows: "Tandem (rex) ad oppidum Canusii in quo morati sumus, cum paucis advenit. Ibique per triduum ante portam, deposito omni regio cultu, miserabiliter, utpote discalceatus et laneis indutus, persistens, non prius cum multo fletu apostolicæ miserationis auxilium et consolationem implorare destitit, quam omnes qui ibi aderant ad tantam pietatem et compassionis misericordiam movit: ut, pro eo multis precibus et lacrymis intercedentes, omnes quidem insolitam nostræ mentis duritiam mirarentur, nonnulli vero, in nobis non apostolicæ severitatis gravitatem, sed quasi tyrannicæ feritatis crudelitatem esse clamarent. Denique instantia compunctionis ejus, et tanto omnium qui ibi aderant supplicatione devicti, tandem eum, relaxato anathematis vinculo, in communionis gratiam et sinum S. Matris Ecclesiæ recipimus; acceptis ab eo securitatibus quæ inferius scriptæ sunt." *Regest.*, Lib. IV. Ep. 12, *ad Germanos.* A monkish annalist, Lambert of Hertzfeld, related the scene in his *Annales:* "Venit ille (Heinricus), ut jussum fuerat, et cum castellum illud triplici muro septum esset, intra secundum, murorum ambitum receptus, foris derelicto omni comitatu suo, deposito cultu regio, nihil præferens regium, nihil ostentans pompaticum, nudis pedibus jejunus a mane usque ad vesperam perstabat, Romani Pontificis sententiam præstolando. Hoc secundo, hoc tercio die fecit. Quarto demum die in conspectum ejus admissus, post multas hinc inde dictas sententias, his postremo conditionibus excommunicatione absolutus est." Pertz, *Monumenta Germaniæ historica*, Vol. VII.—*Lamberti Annales*, Anno 1077. See also Milman, *History of Latin Christianity*, Vol. IV. pp. 96 et seq.

treason could break down his courage. The perfidy alone of a son succeeded in doing so. But the successors of Hildebrand saw the heroic race of Hohenstaufen rise up before them in opposition; and even if, under the axe of the executioner, the head of the last representative of this glorious family should have rolled from the scaffold, their resistance had lasted long enough to render the establishment of the universal monarchy of the popes a thing for ever impossible.

An annalist calls Gregory VII. *præceptor impossibilium.* The great pontiff had been able to ascertain for himself that his designs could not all be realized. He had no doubt seen an Emperor of Germany implore, during three days, pardon for his faults; but in turn he succumbed, and it was far from the Eternal City that he breathed his last, denied by his subjects, and forsaken by his party. Henry IV. had taken his revenge for Canossa; he had again caused Gregory VII. to be deposed, had led his anti-pope, Clement III., to Rome, and had caused himself to be consecrated King of Italy.

Gregory VII. personifies the Papacy. It will, therefore, be of use to examine his doctrines more closely. The primordial idea is well known. According to the Catholic view there are in man two distinct and hostile elements, —the soul and the body. Now, in the organization of society, what represents the soul? The Church. And what represents the body? Lay society. The life of lay society, the State, is not then the true life, and humanity cannot gain salvation without submitting to the direction of the Church.

The manner in which Gregory VII. set forth his theory is interesting in more than one respect. His bulls, his letters, his *dictatus*, the authenticity of which has been vainly contested, show us how he understood his distinction of the two powers (*k*). "The name of the Pope,"

(*k*) Gieseler, *Kirchengeschichte*, Vol. II. Part I. § 23; Part II. § 47.

we read in the *dictatus*, "is unique in the world. He can depose emperors, he can absolve subjects from their oath of fidelity." The letters of Gregory VII. are equally categorical. "The Chair of St. Peter has the right to bind and loose things spiritual. Much more then has it power over things temporal." It is a direct power, which the Pope pretends to exercise; it is an absolute power, which according to his own declarations he possesses. The ideas of Gregory VII. on the respective positions of the two powers, spiritual and temporal, are not less formal. One of his letters makes it known to us in a striking manner, and were it not for the thought of the incalculable evils brought on the world by the pontifical ambition, one would be tempted to admire such pride, such haughty confidence. "Kings," says the greatest of all the popes, "have their origin from men, who inspired by the devil, seek to rule over their fellows. They are urged on by blind ambition and intolerable presumption. The means by which they seek their end are rapine, perfidy, homicide, and all imaginable crimes. It is these polluted men who seek to bow to their feet the Anointed of the Lord. This pretension calls to mind the prince of the fallen angels, Satan, who tempted the Son of God by promising Him the kingdoms of the world, *All these things will I give thee if thou wilt worship me*. Must not a dignity invented by men, who know not God, be subject to a dignity which Providence has created for its own honour, and has given to the world in mercy?" Thus temporal power comes from Satan, spiritual power from God; civil power is born of the devil, ecclesiastical power is of heavenly origin.

Facts gave a stern denial to the proud Hildebrand. We have seen that he failed in his struggle against Henry IV. William the Conqueror had scornfully rejected his demands. At the synod of Winchester (1076), Gregory's law prescribing the celibacy of the clergy was very materially modified; the bishops whom he had summoned to Rome were refused leave of absence; the king continued to exercise the right of investiture. The presumptuous demands of the Pope were answered with cold indifference. "Hubertus legatus tuus," so wrote the king, "religiose pater, ad me veniens ex tua parte me admonuit, quatenus tibi et successoribus tuis fidelitatem facerem, et de pecunia, quam antecessores mei ad Romanam Ecclesiam mittere solebant, melius cogitarem. Unum admisi, alterum non admisi. Fidelitatem facere nolui, nec volo: quia nec ego promisi, nec antecessores meos antecessoribus tuis id fecisse comperio" (*l*). Elsewhere also Gregory's efforts met with want of success. Nevertheless there is one thing to be remarked; however violent, however haughty might be his pretensions, they penetrated into the general conscience of humanity. As Bluntschli has pointed out, from the time of Gregory VII. the Pope takes the very highest rank. In the opinion of Christendom, he takes his place even above the imperial throne. The resistance of Germany has been able to prevent the formation of a universal ecclesiastical monarchy, but it was not possible to retain the jurisdiction of the emperors over the popes. The emperors have had to content themselves with shaking off the papal supremacy; they have not possessed the power requisite for re-establishing the sovereignty of the State over the Papacy; and an impression was formed that the Pope was the first sovereign of Christianity and that the other sovereigns owed him homage (*m*).

This is the great victory of Gregory VII.; this is his title to the eternal gratitude of the Roman Church. Whatever may be, in other respects, thought of his plans, it is not possible to resist bowing before his grandeur of mind. "This most mighty spirit, a character almost without equal," says Gregorovius, "does not stand in

(*l*) Baronius, *Annales*, Anno 1079, No. XXV.; *Guillelmi R. Ep. ad Gregorium.*

(*m*) Bluntschli, *De la responsabilité et de l'irresponsabilité du Pape dans le droit international.* Translated from the German by A. Rivier.

the fair rank of sages and reformers to whom all nations without distinction look up as benefactors of the earth. His aspect awakes admiration, yet not the fire of enthusiasm for a creative ideal, or the general power of a world-appeasing sensibility. A place belongs to him among the mighty of the earth who have constrained the world by force, though agitating it in a salutary manner. But the religious element raises him into a far higher sphere than that of earthly monarchs. Beside him Napoleon sinks down far into a poverty of ideas. Gregory VII. was also heir of the old aim of the Papacy. But the unparalleled genius of the ruler and statesman is his own, and no man has attained to his revolutionary boldness either in ancient Rome or in later times. His fearful war-cry in the strife against temporal tyranny for which he wished to substitute spiritual, *maledictus homo, qui prohibet gladium suum a sanguine*, expresses his inexorable nature. . . . . The genial power by which Gregory VII. gained the freedom of the Church and founded the domination of the hierarchy is astonishing. The empire of priests who bear no other weapons in their hands than a cross and a gospel, a blessing and a curse, is more worthy of wonder than all the empires of Roman or Asiatic conquerors." The illustrious writer adds, "The best thing that Gregory did was the awakening of mind in the world by a contest, which, for the first time, penetrated into all the moral depths of life. This one man excited an immeasureable movement in all circles of Church and State. The gigantic struggle of both these forms which represent the social whole, their barbarous feudal admixture at first, their temporary separation, their lasting strain, constitutes the great mental life of the middle ages, and even at the present day it is a question how to set forth Church and State as fully free, to deliver them from their last hierarchical rigidity, to equalize them by common principles of freedom and love, to make them social, and so for the first time to construct the universal empire of culture and peace" (*n*).

The successors of Gregory took up his theories, and the canon law confirms them in numerous pages. It will not, perhaps, be without interest, to cite some of these affirmations (*o*).

The decretal *Venerabilem* of Innocent III. is dated 1202. Henry VI. had died in 1197. The majority of the electors had chosen Philip of Swabia as his successor; the minority, Otho of Brunswick. Both competitors were proclaimed, but Innocent claimed to call Otho to the throne, Philip having been excommunicated. A legate was sent to Germany. The Princes, who supported the Emperor, protested. The Pope on his side replied by the bull *Venerabilem*.

It contains five propositions, namely:—

1. The right of electors is derived from the Pope.
2. The Pope has the right to examine, and therefore to reject, the elect whom he is called on to consecrate and crown.
3. An improper choice of the majority gives the Pope the power of sanctioning the choice of the minority.
4. The excommunication and personal offences of the elect, as well as the excommunication of his ancestors, make him unworthy.
5. To the Pope belongs the right of absolving from an oath, whether lawfully or unlawfully administered.

A bull of Innocent III., dated 15th August, 1215, annuls and quashes the Magna Charta extorted by the English barons from John Lackland. The Pope represents the undertaking of the barons as the work of the devil; instead of revolting against their king, they ought to have attracted to them his benevolence by proofs of

(*n*) Gregorovius, *Geschichte der Stadt Rom im Mittelalter*, Vol. IV. pp. 249 et seq.

(*o*) Sir Robert Phillimore, *International Law*, Vol. II. pp. 317 et seq.; Daunou, *Essai sur la puissance temporelle des Papes*.

humility. He characterizes as vile and shameful the act forced on John Lackland. "Set up above the nations and above kingdoms in order to root out and to destroy, to plant and to build," he says, "we do not wish to suffer any longer so daring a wickedness which tends to contempt of the Apostolic See, to the detriment of the rights of the king, and to the opprobrium of the English nation. In consequence, in the name of the Almighty God, by the authority of the Apostles Saint Peter and Saint Paul, and by our own, we reprove and condemn this charter; we forbid under pain of anathema that the king shall observe it, or that the barons shall require its execution; we declare null and we quash the charter and all obligations entered into in order to confirm it: we will that in no case it shall have any force."

The decretal *Ad Apostolicæ* pronounces the deposition of the Emperor Frederic II. by the sentence of Pope Innocent IV. and the advice of the Council of Lyons. His subjects are freed from their oath of fidelity; those who profess to remain attached to their sovereign are excommunicated. The Pope founds his right of deposition on the words of Christ: "*Quodcumque ligaveris super terram, ligatum erit et in cœlis.*"

The decretal *Clericis laicos* is the work of Boniface VIII. The Third and Fourth Lateran Councils had ruled that the State has no authority over the goods of the Church. Boniface VIII. proclaims this principle against Philippe le Bel, who claimed the power of taxing the clergy in order to defray the expenses of the war against England. He excommunicated those who impose taxes and those who pay them.

Boniface VIII. published, in 1302, the celebrated bull *Unam sanctam*, in which he enunciates his arrogant theories: "The Church is one; it is a single body which has only one head, and not two like a monster. This single head is Jesus Christ and St. Peter, His vicar, and the successor of St. Peter . . . . We learn by the Gospel that in this Church and under His power are two swords,—the spiritual and the temporal; the one should be employed by the Church and by the hand of the Pontiff, the other by the Church and by the hand of the kings and of the warriors by order and permission of the Pontiff. Now, it is necessary that the one sword should be subject to the other, that the temporal power be subject to the spiritual; otherwise they will not be ordered, and they ought to be as the Apostle says. According to the testimony of truth the spiritual power ought to inspire the temporal power and to judge it if it go astray. Thus is verified in respect to the Church the prophecy of Jeremiah: *I have established thee over the nations and the kingdoms.* But if the Church has the right of judging kings, God alone can judge the spiritual power. Then whoever resists the Church, resists God. To deny that princes are subject to the Church is to admit two principles, like the Manicheans." The conclusion is that it is necessary to salvation that every human creature be subject to the Pope: "*Porro subesse Romano Pontifici omni humanæ creaturæ declaramus, definimus et pronunciamus omnino esse de necessitate salutis.*" The reception which Philippe le Bel reserved for the Papal declaration is well known. He caused Guillaume de Nogaret to pronounce a violent act of requisition against Boniface, convoked the States General, and appealed to the future Council and future Pope as to all that Boniface could do.

Clement V., who in his bull *Meruit* had softened down the bull *Unam Sanctam*, affirmed the pretended rights of the Holy See in the decretal *Romani Principes.*

The climax of the Papal pretensions was reached in the Extravagant *De consuetudine* of John XXII. It is important from the point of view of international law. "The Pope," as we read there, "is placed by God over all kingdoms, and as he cannot go everywhere, he has need of lieutenants or legates to exercise his powers over the nations committed to his care; some nations have in truth pre-tented that legates cannot be sent to them against their will; this is a claim which is inadmissible and deserving of condemnation, and the attempt to exercise such a right draws down immediate excommunication upon the whole country."

Let us refer to one last document, the bull *In cœna Domini* or *Pastoralis.*

It is difficult to ascertain precisely the date of its appearance. It is said to have been published, in a very simple form, for the first time in 1372. Since then it has been promulgated at Rome every year on Holy Thursday, and, by a special provision, the fact of its publication at Rome merely was sufficient to make it obligatory all over the world. Gregory XII. modified it in 1411. Pius V., and afterwards Paul V., gave it a new character. Urban VIII. at last brought it to its final form. The bull *In cœna Domini* ought to serve as an eternal law to Christendon, and above all to bishops, penitentiaries and confessors, who ought, in the confessional, to engrave it deeply on the hearts of all. It excommunicates and curses all heretics and schismatics, all who give them shelter, who favour or defend them; and consequently all princes and magistrates who authorize heretics to sojourn in their States. It excommunicates and curses all those who, without the permission of the Pope, keep or print the books of heretics, all those who appeal from the decisions of Rome to a future general council, whether they be individuals, universities, or other corporations. It intermeddles with the autonomy of the State, and interferes with the right of the State to raise imposts, establish tolls, and exercise justice. It claims the right of punishing crimes against religion. The Pope, unless when on his death-bed, is the only one who can grant freedom from its censures.

This bull excited general opposition, and there is not a country where the civil authority, which it treated so outrageously, has not been opposed to its publication. In

France the Parliament of Paris ordained, in 1580, that every bishop or archbishop, who shall publish it, should be accused of high treason, and should be liable to confiscation of his goods; an *Arrêt* of the sovereign council of Roussillon, of 22nd March, 1763, declared it contrary to the holy canons, to the liberties of the Gallican Church, to the maxims of the kingdom, and to the royal authority. "The bull *In cœna Domini*," said Cappot, Advocate-General to the council, in his discourse, "contains almost as many attempts against the power of sovereigns, and against our manners in particular, and against our maxims, as it contains provisisions. The king would be king in name only, if it were executed" (*p*). The Viceroy of Naples was at times equally opposed to its publication in his States. Rodolph II. solemnly protested against its publication in Germany and in Bohemia. The Archbishop of Mayence showed himself quite as inflexible. So also Venice. Spain renewed the prohibition down to 1762. Finally Clement XIII. having in 1768 appealed to this celebrated document, in support of a brief, which he had issued against the Duke of Parma, all the Catholic States vied with each other in protesting. Since Clement XIV., the bull is no longer read, as formerly, at Rome on every Holy Thursday; but the Roman Church still considers it as a legislative act in force in its tribunals and congregations.

Rome tried to put in practice the principles formulated by its pontiffs. We have seen Gregory VII. at work. His successors followed his example; but they also exhausted themselves in vain efforts. Temporary triumphs could not prevent final defeat. In the 13th century the Papacy overcame the powerful family of Hohenstaufen; yet it was obliged in the 14th century to abandon the Eternal City. Boniface VIII. had been the last great

(*p*) Durand de Maillane, *Les libertés de l'Eglise gallicane prouvées et commentées*, Vol. I. p. 322.

Pope, and those who after him ascended the chair of St. Peter were for a long time only tools of the ambition of the kings.

The contest besides had become unequal. Under Gregory VII. the faithful had taken part for the Pope and against the emperor. Under Innocent III. popular opinion had forced Phillip Augustus to yield. The accusation of heresy hurled against Frederic II. had yet power enough to turn popular opinion against a race illustrious for heroism. In the 14th century, on the contrary, we see the kings, in their contests with the Holy See, receive support from the people. In France, the first States General were convoked by Philippe le Bel to oppose the attempts of Boniface VIII., and it was in rallying around their king against the haughty pretensions of Rome that the French first became conscious of their nationality. Germany acted like France; in March, 1339, the princes and states of the empire passed the decree of the Diet of Frankfort, thus confirming the imperial ordonnances of 8th August, 1338, and their own declarations that "the emperor holds all his power from God, that once chosen he needs neither confirmation nor coronation from the Pope;" and they proclaimed guilty of high treason "whosoever shall maintain the contrary."

In England the exercise of the Papal power had always been contested, and the public law of this country furnishes many documents passed into law with a view to resist Rome. The Constitutions of Clarendon of 1164 and of 1246, the Statute of Carlisle of 1307, the Articles of the Clergy of 1340 and 1344, the Statutes of Provisors of 1350, 1363 and 1389, the Statutes of Præmunire of 1391 and 1392, are so many examples. By the 27 Edw. III. c. 1, "all the people of the king's liegeance, which shall draw any out of the realm in plea, whereof the cognizance pertaineth to the king's court, or of things whereof judgments be given in the king's court, or which do sue in any other court, to defeat or impeach the judgments given in the king's court, shall have a day containing the space of two months, by warning to be made to them, to appear before the king and his council, or in his chancery, or before the king's justices of the one bench or the other, to answer to the king for contempt. And if they come not at the day, to be at the law, they, their procurators, attornies, executors, notaries, and maintainers shall be put out of the king's protection, and their lands and goods forfeit to the king, and their bodies (wheresoever they may be found) shall be taken and imprisoned, and ransomed at the king's will: and upon the same a writ shall be made to take them by their bodies, and to seize their lands and goods into the king's hands; and if it be returned that they be not found, they shall be put in exigent and outlawed." By the Statute of *Præmunire*, 16 Rich. II. c. 5, if any shall purchase or pursue, in the court of Rome or elsewhere, any processes, sentences of excommunication, bulls or instruments, against any persons executing judgments in the king's court, or shall bring within the realm or receive the same, he shall be put out of the king's protection, his lands and goods forfeited to the king, and shall be attached by his body if he may be found, and brought before the king and his council there to answer, or else process to be made against him by *præmunire facias* as in other statutes of provisors. In the 16th century, Henry VIII. only followed the line of conduct pursued by his predecessors; and, by the advice of the most profound English lawyers, the numerous statutes made by parliament during his reign are *declaratory* only of the ancient law of the realm.

The pretensions of the Papacy were condemned by the facts. The divine right which the Papacy claimed in spiritual matters was to be equally called in question. In this point of view the Councils of Constance and of Basle form a real revolution in the Church. Christendom proclaimed itself sovereign, and would see in the popes merely the ministers of its will; to such a result did the policy of the great pontiffs of the Middle Ages tend. The popes, without doubt, did not abandon their haughty claims. At certain periods we shall see them renewed with greater audacity than in the past; but, do as they might, the world has shaken off even the moral supremacy which the popes exercised on it. Thanks to the efforts of Gregory VII. the idea of the supreme rank of the Papacy had taken root in the human mind. In the 16th century this notion entirely disappeared. New ideas made way for themselves, and the ideal of the Middle Ages, the false conception of Christian unity—one God, one Pope, one Emperor, the words are those of Frederic Barbarossa—will be replaced by an ideal more noble, more lofty and more true.

II.

Before examining the international position of the spiritual Papacy since the Reformation, we must say some words of its mode of representation in the Middle Ages, and of certain diplomatic acts—the Pragmatic Sanctions and the Concordats (*q*).

The custom of sending out to the Churches representatives of the Pope goes back very far. The Council of Sardica even gives us a formal text, "Quod si is, qui rogat causam suam iterum audiri, deprecatione sua moverit episcopum Romanum, ut de latere suo presbyteros mittat, erit in potestate ejus. . . . ."

Numerous delegations were made; and except in the East they were not generally refused. Still later, the See of Rome maintained at the court of Constantinople a permanent delegate, the *Apocrisarius*.

In the Middle Ages, the first legates were sent *ad visi-*

(*q*) Thomassin, *Vetus ac nova Ecclesiæ disciplina*, Pars I. Lib. II. Cap. 117; Ferraris, *Bibliotheca canonica*, Ed. nova, 1840, art. *Legatus;* Herzog, *Real-Encyclopädie für protestantische Theologie und Kirche*, art. *Legaten und Nuncien der Römischen Kirche;* Moroni, *Dizionario di erudizione storico-ecclesiastica*, art. *Nunzio apostolico*; Rotteck and Welcker, *Staats-Lexikon*, art. *Nuncien*.

tandas ecclesias by Leo IX. and Victor II. From the time of Gregory VII. their missions were multiplied, and their exactions, their scandalous abuses form one of the darkest chapters of the history of Catholicism. Their haughty pride, their insulting arrogance, called everywhere protestations, and there was not one prince, perhaps, who did not stipulate that legates should not enter his States without his permission. The kings of France and of England defended their sovereign rights with real obstinacy. William II. of England made a convention with Pope Urban II. "ne legatus Romanus ad Angliam mitteretur nisi quem rex præciperet." Henry III. maintained this prerogative, which we see fully recognized from 1187, as belonging to Scotland. In Germany the Hohenstaufens were equally resolute.

According to the canon law (*De officio legati*, in the Decretals of Gregory IX., l. I., tit. 30; l. VI., tit. 15) there are:

First. The *Legati à latere.* They are ordinary or extraordinary, according as they are sent into a province or only sent at the time of some extraordinary occurrence. They are Cardinals. They are invested with every jurisdiction; they are, as they are named, the Ordinaries of the Ordinaries in the provinces given into their charge, and have all the powers of patriarchs, primates, archbishops, bishops, and other ordinaries. They have not the powers formally excepted, and reserved to the Pope. The Council of Trent expressly forbids them, as well as other legates, to disturb bishops in the exercise of their jurisdiction in causes belonging to the ecclesiastical tribunal, or to proceed against clerks without the requisition of the bishops, unless the bishop neglects to punish.

Second. The *Legati missi* or *nuncii apostolici.* They are divided into two clases: some are *primi ordinis*, others *secundi ordinis.*

Third. The *Legati nati.* The dignity is attached to the See, and not to the Prelate. Such were the archbishops of Canterbury, York, Rheims, Salzburg, Cologne, and Prague.

All legates have an ordinary jurisdiction in the provinces entrusted to them, but this jurisdiction is greater or less, according to the rank they occupy. We have seen the powers of the legate *à latere*. He can give absolution even for the murder of a clerk, he can confirm the election of bishops, he can confer benefices. The *legatus missus* has less extensive rights. Thus with respect to benefices he can grant those only which do not exceed in value twenty-four ducats. All apostolic envoys can grant indulgences varying in length from 100 days to a whole year; to chapels and churches they can grant indulgences of seven years and seven times forty days. They have the examination of persons to be promoted in cathedral churches. We shall soon see the danger, which this confusion of the religious and political character involved.

The Pragmatic Sanctions and the Concordats divide themselves into three groups. The first is anterior to the Reformation, and is connected with the great councils of the 15th century. The French Concordat of 1516 is the last instance. The second group took place in the last century. The third began in 1801 (*r*).

Bluntschli has very well pointed out the special nature of the conventions which have intervened in spiritual affairs between Rome and the different governments (*s*). They are not treaties properly so called, for the Pope does not sign them as king but as head of the Church. Yet the principles relating to treaties are by analogy applied to these conventions. But in this application great circumspection must be used. International law can in reality only imperfectly protect Concordats. On the one hand the contracting State can use all the means authorized by law, and may even have recourse to violence; on the other

(*r*) Sir Robert Phillimore, *International Law*, Vol. II. pp. 375 et seq.

(*s*) Bluntschli, *Das moderne Völkerrecht der civilisirten Staten*, Book VI. art. 443.

hand, the Church, if she does not possess these means, can use those which religious authority grants her, and which are not placed under the control of international law. The obligatory force of Concordats is also of a distinct nature. They are only temporary regulations, made by common agreement, of the relations between the Church and the State on the frontiers where these move about, and frequently enter into conflict. In principle the State is as much authorized to regulate these questions alone and without the concurrence of the Church as the Church is to make religious resolutions. This right of both parties is not lost by Concordats. The Roman Canonists even have never ceased to claim for the Pope the right of derogating from concluded conventions (*t*). That which is allowed in favour of the development of religious life must be granted for political motives to civil society. In short, it should be firmly impressed on the mind that Concordats cease to be obligatory as soon as one of the contracting parties refuse to respect them any longer.

The first in date of the Concordats is the celebrated Concordat of Worms, concluded in 1122, between Calixtus II. and the Emperor Henry V. The emperor relinquished the right of investiture by the ring and the crosier, and granted freedom of ecclesiastical elections on condition that they were made in his presence. It was agreed that the elect should receive from him the regalia, and should fulfil their bounden duties. It is a characteristic fact that the Concordat of Worms was found fault with by the zealous men of the papal party. It was in reality a deviation from the system of Gregory VII., who wished to break every tie of dependance between the clergy and civil society, to displace the power which granted investiture, and to take investiture from the empire in order to give it to the Papacy. Whereas the Concordats sanction the

(*t*) Richter, *Lehrbuch des katholischen und evangelischen Kirchenrechts*, § 88; O. Mejer, *Zur Geschichte der römisch-deutschen Frage*; Id., *Lehrbuch des Kirchenrechts*, pp. 132 et seq.

political dependance of the clergy, and left to the empire a powerful means of influence on the temporalities of churches, and thereby even over the spiritualities.

One of the most important diplomatic instruments is the Pragmatic Sanction of March, 1268. It is the work of St. Louis, and is directed against Rome. It is not then a convention made between the Holy See and France; and if we refer to it, it is because it, as well as the Pragmatic Sanction of Bourges of 1438, gave rise to endless negotiations between Rome and the crown of France. The Pragmatic Sanction of 1268 secured the liberty of ecclesiastical elections, prohibited the collecting of any tribute for the profit of the Church of Rome without permission from the king, and proclaimed that the kingdom of France "has always been held from God alone." The Pragmatic Sanction of 1438, the work of Charles VII., determined the authority of General Councils, and laid down rules for the collation of benefices, abolishing by one blow apostolic reservatives, expectatives, and annats. It is, in short, the application to the Gallican Church of the decrees of the Council of Basle (*u*).

The Concordat of Vienna was concluded, 17th February, 1448, between Nicolas V. and the Emperor Frederic III., and confirmed the triumph of the Papacy over the Council of Basle. France had supported the decrees of the Council of Basle. England at first neutral and undecided, had neglected to take up a position. Germany ended by being gained to the Roman cause. The Concordat of Vienna put the Pope into possession of the nominations to a great number of benefices, and completed a partition of interest between the German princes and Rome.

The Pragmatic Sanction of Bourges was soon the point aimed at by the attacks of the Papacy. Eugene IV. had protested against it. Pius II. renewed the complaints of

(*u*) Portalis, *Discours, rapports et travaux inédits sur le concordat de* 1801, *publiés et précédés d'une introduction par le vicomte Portalis*, Introduction, p. 21.

his predecessors. Louis XI. had even intended to yield, but the Parliament refused to register the letters-patent of abrogation. Paul II. was urgent and pressing. The University of Paris took part in the debate, and declared that it would appeal to a future Council. The king, however, was bent upon making peace with the Pope, and made a treaty in 1472 with Sextus IV., which reduced the Pragmatic, as to beneficiary matters, to the same position as the German Concordats. Yet even here he met with the resistance of Parliament. Under Louis XII., Julius II. cast an interdict on France. The king ordered that the Pragmatic should be observed, and assembled his clergy at Tours. But Francis I. signed, in December, 1515, a Concordat which was ratified by Pope Leo X., 16th March, 1516, and abolished what the Advocate-General of the Parliament, Jean de St. Roman, had so justly called the Palladium of France. Pope and king divided between them the spoils of the Gallican Church. The annates were re-established in exchange for these concessions, and the king obtained the right of nomination to ecclesiastical benefices.

III.

The Reformation finished the destruction of the work of the Middle Ages. In Protestant countries it took from the Church the base of her domination, by putting an end to the dualism of life, to the hostility of body and of soul of spiritual and temporal life. In politics it broke down the false unity of Catholicism by recognizing the principle of individual and national sovereignty. The superiority of the priest over the layman was overthrown; spiritual power was no more; each nation was to be sovereign, and the sovereignty should extend to things spiritual as well as to things temporal; the priesthood was to be no longer either outside of the State, nor above the

State, but was to be within the State. New changes took place with respect to the international situation of the Papacy. Henceforth, it is true, the Pope had the sovereignty of the Pontifical States, and thus had a right to the privileges of international law. But from his double character as head of the Church and as sovereign, the Protestant princes only imperfectly acknowledged his right to these privileges, while in even the most Catholic countries his pretensions forced the civil power to resist him.

The popes of the Middle Ages had tried to arrogate to themselves the part of sovereign arbiters of the world,—they had wished to have themselves recognized as masters of the nations. Even on the eve of the Reformation, Alexander VI. promulgated his decision relative to the New World, and, before him, Urban IV. had given to the king of Bohemia all the lands of the infidels, the inhabitants of which should be converted by his means, or which he should have conquered; while Nicholas V. had granted the king of Portugal the power of invading the lands of all infidels, and of reducing their persons to servitude. But such facts will no longer present themselves: the claims will be as haughty as before, but the general conscience of humanity will not admit them.

This is not the place to recount the vicissitudes of the struggle. The Reformation at first advanced from triumph to triumph. In the years which followed the religious peace of Augsburg of 1555, the Evangelical Church appeared everywhere victorious. The north and centre of Germany belonged to it. It seemed certain that it would also have the south. The States of Austria, of Styria, and of Carinthia, were gained by it. The Hussite movement of Bohemia and Moravia joined itself in these countries to the movement of the Reformation. All the Imperial cities were Protestant. In Switzerland, the superiority of the new religion was incontestable. The nobility and people of Poland were detached from Rome.

The same thing was to be seen in Sweden and Norway. In England, the work of Henry VIII. and Edward VI. was decidedly crowned with success. The Low Countries were the theatre of a courageous and active propaganda. In France, the Huguenots extracted by force the peace of St. Germain, and Calvinist communities were seen to arise even in Italy itself. Now, what was the result? After some time, Catholicism is seen to regain a part of the lost ground. An internal reformation, a new affirmation of its principles, an incessant activity against the enemy, —such are the factors of the reaction. The popes, the Catholic princes, and, above all, the Company of Jesus, did the rest.

The religious wars of the sixteenth century furnish us with many instances of the depositions of princes declared by the Pope in virtue of his pretended superiority. In 1535, Paul III. excommunicated Henry VIII., forbid his subjects to obey him, ordered his nobles to revolt against him, and required all bishops and pastors to leave England, which was placed under interdict. In 1558, Paul IV. excommunicated and deprived of their kingdoms all heretic princes present and to come. Pius V. fulminated a bull against Queen Elizabeth in 1570, dethroning her and ordering her subjects to rise against her. This bull was renewed by Gregory XIII. and Sextus V. This last excommunicated Henry IV., declared him deprived of his kingdom of Navarre, and disqualified and incapable of succeeding to the kingdom of France. Gregory XIV. repeated the anathemas of his predecessor. The real effect scarcely corresponded to these arrogant decrees: England remained faithful to her princes, and in France we see the parliaments deliver to the executioner the bulls of the Holy See.

The Thirty Years' War gave a great blow to the Papacy, and the peace of Westphalia made, in theory at least, tolerance a law of the European world. The Court of Rome had neglected nothing to make the negociations abortive. The papal legates had the voices of the ecclesiastical states at their disposal, and they delayed to the last moment every kind of concession. When they saw the emperor himself forced to give way, they tried to weaken the peace by placing restrictions on the equality of the confessions and by excluding from the peace the Calvinists and Anabaptists (*x*). Nothing came of it. But two days after the signature of the treaty, the Nuncio Chigi deposited a protest, and, 20th November, 1648, appeared the bull *Zelo domus Dei*, which annulled the treaty, "Potestatis plenitudine penitus damnamus, reprobamus, cassamus, annullamus viribus et effectu vacuamus." At Vienna, the Nuncio even tried to excite the people against the treaty. He did not succeed, but nevertheless contrived to induce the Emperor to exclude the religious peace from his hereditary states. The Holy See persevered so well in its attitude that in 1782 the Curia replied to Prussia, who had retrenched herself behind the treaty of 1648, that the Holy See had never recognized this treaty.

The Papacy came out of the wars of the sixteenth and seventeenth centuries with diminished importance. Accordingly, it is no longer seen since then to take a preponderating position in the affairs of the world. Its theories remained those of the Papacy of the Middle Ages, but the feeble successors of the pontiffs of genius of the eleventh, twelfth, and thirteen centuries were satisfied with carrying on, for the realization of their dreams, a propaganda, active no doubt, mischievous in almost all respects, but, on the whole, ineffectual. Their intrigues, their culpable artifices, their agitations, were able to delay progress, to cause in some countries great evils, but not to prevent the advance of civilization. International law would not even have had to occupy itself with this obscure contest, if the most powerful instruments engaged in it had not been the nuncios.

(*x*) Laurent, *Etudes sur l'histoire de l'humanité*, Tome X., *Les nationalités*, pp. 281 et seq.

The Church, and therefore the Papacy also, claims to have jurisdiction over all who have received baptism. Schismatics and heretics are subordinate to her. Baptism administered by schismatics and heretics is a sacrament. The Council of Trent is explicit on this point: "Si quis dixerit, Baptismum qui etiam datur ab hereticis in nomine Patris et Filii et Spiritus Sancti, cum intentione faciendi quod facit Ecclesia, non esse verum Baptismum: anathema sit" (*y*). A bull of Benedict XIV. to the Polish bishops states this principle in express terms. Pius VI. is equally explicit. "Discrimen intercedit," he writes in 1791 to Cardinal de la Rochefoucauld, "inter homines qui extra gremium Ecclesiæ semper fuerunt, quales sunt Infideles atque Judæi, atque inter illos qui se Ecclesiæ ipsi per susceptum baptismi sacramentum subjecerunt. Primi etenim constringi ad catholicam obedientiam profitendam non debent: contrà vero alteri sunt cogendi." Pius VII. formally reserved to himself all authority over Protestants. In 1803 the question whether a German Catholic might marry a Protestant *divorcée* was laid before him. The answer was in the negative. "According to Holy Scripture, the Councils and tradition," says the Pope, "heretics remain subject to the laws of the Catholic Church" (*z*). In the instructions addressed to the Nuncio of Vienna, in 1805, the same idea is found, which is so truly Roman, that in the famous letter addressed by Pius IX. to the Emperor of Germany, 7th August, 1873, the head of the Catholic Church claims that "whoever has received baptism belongs to the Pope" (*a*).

This theory being admitted, Rome divides the world into two parts: *provincie che dipendano dalla S. Cong. di Propaganda Fide*, and *provincie che dipendano dalla S. Sede*.

(*y*) Trid. Sess. 7, Can. 4, *de Bapt.*

(*z*) O. Mejer, *Die Propaganda, ihre Provinzen, und ihr Recht*, Vol. I. p. 11.

(*a*) The letter is reproduced in many publications, among others in the book entitled: *Nouvelle législation prussienne, réglant les rapports entre l'Etat et l'Eglise*; Berlin, 1874.

To the one, faithful to the Holy See, the normal law of Christendom applies; but to the other, hostile to the Holy See, a law modified according to circumstances (*b*). In the *Provinces of the Holy See*, all the efforts of the Papacy tend to preserve the faith intact; the Church claims the right of ruling alone and without contest: "Fides nostra catholica sine qua impossibile est placere Deo," says a decree of the Council of Trent (*c*). In the *Provinces of the Propaganda*, Rome has only one object and aim: to re-establish true religion.

Thus, the destruction of heresy by fire and sword is justified. Already in the Middle Ages, the bishop exercised the power of inquisition; he was the *inquisitor natus*, as the canon law calls him. Beside this inquisition was placed the inquisition of special delegates of the Papacy. Then followed, in some countries, a special inquisition. Finally, when the Reformation threatened Catholicism with destruction, Paul III. instituted a special congregation for the inquisition, over which the Pope presides by right, and the power of which Pius IV., Pius V. and Sextus V. enlarged. But the inquisition is only an ecclesiastical tribunal; it requires the assistance of the secular arm. What then happens when the State is not Catholic? In that case it is necessary to bring it back to the true faith, by every means to attach it to Rome. A special congregation was organized for this end—the Congregation of the Propaganda.

The Congregation of the Propaganda dates from 1622; it already existed in embryo under Gregory XIII. A decree of this Pope charges "a body of cardinals with the direction of missions in the East," and gives orders "for the printing of catechisms in the less known languages." Yet the institution was neither founded nor furnished with

(*b*) O. Mejer, *Die Propaganda*, Vol. I. pp. 93 et seq.

(*c*) Trid. Sess. 5, *Decr. de peccat. origin.* The *Professio Fidei Tridentinæ* says also: *Catholica fides extra quam nemo salvus esse potest.*

the necessary means, nor even very comprehensive (*d*). In 1613, a Spanish monk, superior of the Discalced Carmelites in Belgium, proposed to the reigning Pope to institute a vast office, from which a uniform action should go forth against non-Catholics. Gregory XV., the first pupil of the Jesuits who mounted the Pontifical throne, the Pope who canonized Ignatius de Loyola and Francis Xavier, realized the idea. The bull of erection is dated 21st June, 1622. Two other decrees completed the institution, and Urban VIII. finished the work of his predecessor.

The functionaries of the Congregation of the Propaganda are the prefects, the vicars apostolic and the bishops; immediately under their orders are the coadjutors, the vicars-general and capitulars, and pro-vicars; beside them come the archbishops, the nuncios and the apostolic visitors and delegates. The vicars apostolic, representing the Pope, are sent into countries where the episcopal hierarchy would not be admitted, *ubi sedes episcoporum impeditæ sunt* (*e*). The fact that the Nuncios, and above all the permanent Nuncios, are agents and auxiliaries of the Propaganda cannot be called in doubt. The instructions given to the Nuncios, the manner in which they were executed, the language of the Court of Rome completely establish it (*f*).

The double character of the Nuncios, religious and diplomatic, had made them a real danger for the States which received them. In France rigorous measures were taken to protect the independence of the Crown and of the Gallican Church against their undertakings. They were never admitted under any other title than that of mere ambassadors of the temporal power of Rome. In 1591, by letters patent, dated 14th July, Henry IV. ordered the Royal

(*d*) Ranke, *The Popes of Rome*, Vol. II. p. 69.

(*e*) O. Mejer, *Die Propaganda*, Vol. I. pp. 24 et seq.

(*f*) See on this subject the very interesting book of O. Mejer, *Die Propaganda*, Vol. I. pp. 23 et seq., and the indications contained in the work of Cerri, Secretary of the Congregation of the Propaganda under the pontificate of Innocent XI., a work published in London by Richard Steele in 1715.

Parliament sitting at Tours to proceed against a Nuncio of Gregory XIV., who had entered the kingdom without his permission, for he was deputed to the chiefs of the League. On 5th August, it was decreed that the Nuncio should be arrested.

The Nuncio had no tribunal nor any jurisdiction, whether voluntary or contentious; and no employment except near the person of the king, and had no other function in the kingdom. This is so true, that, in 1647, the Pope's Nuncio in France having taken in a document the title of *Nuncio in the whole kingdom of France*, and another Nuncio having taken, in 1663, the title of *Nuncio to the Parliament and Kingdom*, the Parliament rose in arms against this novelty. The Court of Rome, or the Nuncios themselves, from time to time renewed the attempts opposed to the Gallican maxims. But as soon as they have been known, the king's advocates resisted, and they were repressed by several Ordonnances and Arrêts of Parliament. For inquiries as to the life, manners, and doctrines of those who were named to consistorial benefices, which the bishops of France had assumed the power of making, the Council of Trent gave the same power to the Legates and Nuncios. But in France, the bishops always maintained the sole right and power of making these inquiries. Urban VIII. contended that the Ordinaries could not make these inquiries except in the absence of the Legates and Nuncios. But his claim was unavailing. The Pope's Nuncio in France could not give any patents for benefices, nor any dispensations. He could not fulminate the bulls addressed to him; he could not be delegated judge *in partibus* to hear and determine the differences of the subjects of the king, because judges of this sort had to be natives of the kingdom. Neither had he the right of visitation or of correction in monasteries, whether exempt or not exempt. An Arrêt of Parliament of 29th March, 1582, declared abusive a rescript of Gregory XIII. delegating his Nuncio to decide a difference which had arisen between the General of the Franciscans and the Superior and Convent of this Order in Paris. So also the Nuncio could not take cognizance of cases of marriage and other causes.

Pithou is very explicit and precise in his *Libertés de l'Eglise gallicane.* "The Pope does not send to France legates *à latere* with powers to reform, judge, confer, dispense, and such others as are customary to be specified by the bulls of their authority, except at the postulation of the most Christian King or by his consent; and the legate does not use his powers until he has given a promise to the king by writing under his seal, and sworn by his Holy Orders not to use the said faculties in the kingdoms, countries, lands, and lordships of his subjection, except so much and so long as it shall please the king; and so soon as the said legate shall be advertised of his will to the contrary, he shall desist and cease, so that he shall not use the said faculties except in regard of those for which he shall have the consent of the king and conformably to it, without undertaking or doing anything prejudicial to the holy decrees, general councils, franchises, liberties, and privileges of the Gallican Church, and of the universities and public studies of this kingdom. And to this end, the faculties of such legates shall be presented to the Court of Parliament, where they shall be viewed, examined, verified, published, and registered under such modifications as the Court shall see fit to make for the good of the kingdom, according to the which modifications, and not otherwise, shall be judged all the processes and differences which shall occur by reason of this" (Art. 11). In Article 12 is found a provision concerning the Legate of Avignon when his faculties extend beyond "the *Comtat Venaissin*, and lands which the Pope at present enjoys." "Before using his faculties in the country of the obedience and sovereignty of the king, the Legate shall take oath and give similar promise in writing, and especially not to encroach on the secular jurisdiction, nor to draw away the subjects, to interdict or excommunicate the officers of the king, or to do anything against the liberties of the Gallican Church, edicts, customs, statutes, and privileges of the country. And under these modifications, and on condition of them, shall be these faculties and those of his vice-legates verified in the Court of Parliament of Dauphiné and others respectively, for that which is of their jurisdiction, after they have been presented by them with placet and letters of the king."

The Arrêté of 18 Germinal, year X, which authorize the registering of the bulls of Cardinal Caprara, Legate *à latere* of the Holy See, produced again the conditions enumerated in the *Libertés de l'Eglise gallicane* by Pithou, and the Cardinal took an oath to make no attempt on the rights of the government and of the nation. The formula imposed on him even included the liberties of the Gallican Church; but Caprara knew how to evade this part of his engagement. The *Articles organiques* of the Concordat of 1801 declare that no individual calling himself Nuncio, legate, vicar, or commissary apostolic, or dignifying himself with any other title, can, without the authorization of the Government, exercise on French soil or elsewhere any function relating to the affairs of the Gallican Church. In his *Exposition des maximes et des règles consacrées par les articles organiques*, Portalis thus expresses himself on the subject of this regulation: "Without doubt it is the Pope who gives the mission when it relates to a matter within his jurisdiction, and it is carried on in his name; but it is by the permission and under the authority of the sovereign that it is carried on; for no process can be executed in a State without the permission of the public power which rules that State." "Certainly," he adds, "the Pope cannot give his mandatories more power than he has himself. Now, what is the power of the Pope in France? In questions which concern the general body of the Church, that is to say, in questions relating to doctrine, and to the execution of the holy decrees, it doubtless belongs to him to promulgate decisions or solemn instructions;

but these decisions and these instructions cannot be published or executed without the previous authorization of the public power. But in particular private affairs and questions, a distinction is made between those which are administrative and those which are contentious. If they are administrative, the bulls or rescripts made to regulate them are submitted to verification, as are all the bulls and briefs which interest the general body of the Church. If they are contentious, either the Pope is entitled to take cognizance of them in the first instance, or he cannot have cognizance, except in case of appeal. In both cases, according to Articles 45 and 46 of the Liberties of the Gallican Church he must delegate, in France and to French ecclesiastics, the power of deciding the cases which are to be judged. The commission of these ecclesiastics is duly verified before its execution; also we have never recognized the authority or the jurisdiction of the congregations which are held in the Court of Rome" (*g*).

In 1823 the Nuncio of the Pope having directly notified to the bishops the nomination of the new Pope, and having asked for their prayers, the Government protested against this irregularity, and addressed a circular to the bishops reminding them of ancient usages and laws on the matter.

It is in the *permanent Nunciatures* which have been instituted at the end of the 16th century, that the real nature of the diplomatic representation of the Holy See is to be seen. The Nuncios of Vienna, Lucerne, Cologne, Warsaw, and Brussels, functionaries of the Propaganda, and charged to make war on Protestantism, have admirably acquitted themselves of their mission; and when we think of the instruction it would convey, it is to be regretted that a history of Nunciatures has not yet been written.

At the time when they were established, the triumph of Catholicism seemed certain. The Church gained ground in Germany. Many Protestant princes were converted. In France, Henry IV. abjured the reformed religion. The

(*g*) Portalis, *Discours, rapports et travaux inédits sur le concordat de* 1801, *publiés et précédés d'une introduction par le vicomte Portalis*, pp. 16 et seq.

Catholic cause carried all before it in Poland, and the Emperor prepared to crush the Reformation.

Switzerland was chosen first as the scene of action of the new institution (*h*). Charles Borromeo tried to establish a Nunciature there in 1570; but his efforts were at first fruitless, and it was only nine years later that John Francis Buonomi, Bishop of Vercelli, thanks to the manœuvres of the Jesuits, was received at Lucerne. The Pope, it is true, was obliged to recall his too zealous representative; but from 1580 the Nunciature of Lucerne was able to set itself regularly to work.

The Nunciature of Cologne dates from 1583. The apostasy of Archbishop Gebhard Truchsess, and the desire of his successor, Ernest of Bavaria, to see his nephew, aged seventeen, named coadjutor to the Episcopal See, furnished the Curia with an opportunity of founding it.

At Cologne, as at Lucerne, the representatives of the Holy See had the powers of *nuncii missi cum potestate legati à latere*, and, in fact, encroached on Episcopal attributions.

The Nunciature of Vienna goes back to 1513. The first Papal envoy was Laurence Campecci; but it was not really until sixty years later that the post became important (*i*). The Nunciature of Brussels was founded in 1597; that of Poland about the same time. Lastly, that of Munich dates from 1786.

Each of these Nunciatures had under its jurisdiction a part of the neighbouring Protestant countries. Cologne ruled Denmark, Hamburg, Lübeck, a great part of Germany, Alsace, and the Principality of Liege. Vienna, in the same way, watched Germany and the other parts of the Empire. Brussels acted on the Low Countries, England and Ireland; Lucerne on Switzerland and the South of

(*h*) Snell, Glück and Henne, *Pragmatische Erzählung der kirchlichen Ereignisse in der katholischen Schweiz;* Snell, *Geschichte der Einführung der Nuntiatur in der Schweiz;* Vulliemin, *Histoire de la confédération suisse;* O. Mejer, *Die Propaganda*, Vol. II. pp. 107 et seq.

(*i*) In the *Responsio* of Pius VI., the work of Cardinal Campanelli and directed against the German archbishops, is found a complete list of the Nuncios of Vienna from 1513 to 1785.

Germany; Warsaw on Sweden and Norway. This was the manner in which the field of operations was marked out. As to the instructions, they may be guessed without trouble. The Nuncio of Lucerne (1608—1612), Ladislas di Aquino, Bishop of Venafro, says that the end of the Propaganda is the maintenance of Catholicism. Sextus V., in a brief, had already written to a Nuncio that his mission was to convert the heretics. The instructions to the Nuncio Maldeschi are equally precise (*k*).

Each of the Nunciatures seemed to rival the others in zeal, and the Nuncios were so many firebrands of discord in the countries in which they set to work.

In 1594, we already find the Protestants of Germany complain to the Diet of the Empire, and denounce the agitations of the representatives of the Holy See, who, they said, continually attacked the peace of religion. In 1680, the Emperor Leopold I. addressed Pope Innocent XI., declared that the Holy See has not the right of giving its Nuncios a right of jurisdiction, and threatened to break with Rome. In 1598 and in 1645 the German Protestants renewed their remonstrances. The Catholic Episcopate even rose against the encroachments of the Papal envoys. In 1689 the Archbishop of Mayence protested against the conduct of the Nuncio of Cologne, who claimed to exercise his jurisdiction even in Mayence; and the Archbishop of Cologne had to strive at the same time against the Nuncio, who claimed the right of visitation in the diocese of Liege. At every moment, and even in affairs of the very least importance, the representative of the Papacy in Cologne made his voice heard. In 1709, he annulled a convention made between the king of Prussia and the town of Cologne, intended to secure the exercise of his religion by the Prussian envoy, spoke of the Protestant religion as *secta illa damnata*, and obliged the king to propose to the *Corpus Evangelicorum* to request

(*k*) See O. Mejer, *Die Propaganda*, Vol. I. pp. 322 et seq.

the Emperor either to expel the Nuncio, or to oblige him to withdraw his scandalous document, and be more temperate in future. In 1736, the Emperor Charles VI. was obliged to declare to the Pope that he could no longer suffer a Nuncio at Cologne, as the Nuncio was a disturber of the public peace. In 1742, the diet of the Electoral Princes had laid before it a protestation of the Nuncio against the recognition of the Duke of Hanover as Prince Elector, a subject which did not in any way concern him. A frequent cause of conflicts was found besides, in the fact that from the 16th century the Ecclesiastical Princes had let their civil jurisdiction be exercised by their religious officials. The envoys of the Holy See took advantage of this circumstance to judge appeals on every matter. The *Recess* of the Empire for 1654 explicitly forbid them to do so; and the German prelates on their side maintained the rights of the Episcopate with as much courage as vigour, as the events which occurred at the end of the last century sufficiently testify (*l*).

To satisfy the desires of Charles Theodore, Elector Palatine, who aimed at freeing himself from the archiepiscopal jurisdiction, and to extend, at the same time, its own power, the Curia decreed, in 1786, the establishment of a Nunciature at Munich. The measure was a very extensive one. Up to that time, the three Nunciatures of Cologne, Vienna, and Lucerne divided among themselves, in a certain way, central Germany. The titularies of these posts claimed, without doubt, to exercise a vigorous action on the archbishops and bishops. But the new Nunciature was to contain exactly the territories of the Elector Palatine of Bavaria, and was established with the express intention of, as much as possible, excluding the bishops who, up to this time, had been competent in these territories. The movement of resistance was the stronger, as it had long been prepared in the minds of men. The

(*l*) Herzog, *Real-Encyclopädie*, art. *Emser Congress und Punktuation.*

Episcopal system, sprung from the Gallican ideas, had found favour in Germany. Introduced in great part by the great Belgian Canonist, Van Espen, admirably explained and propagated by Nicolas Von Hontheim, Suffragan Bishop of Treves, who wrote under the name of Febronius, it had been welcomed by the German clergy (*m*).

The resistance to the new measure was great. The Archbishops of Treves, Cologne, and Salzburg, answering to the appeal of the Archbishop of Mayence, assembled at Ems, and committed to writing, 25th August, 1786, an act, famous in ecclesiastical annals, in which they resolutely affirmed the rights inherent in the Episcopal dignity, protested against the abuses of power committed by the Popes, and required the abolition of Nunciatures, so far as they had a religious character. The document of Ems was addressed to Joseph II.; the inferior clergy were forbidden to maintain relations either with Zoglio, the new Nuncio of Munich, or with the Nuncio Pacca, then titulary of the diplomatic post of Cologne. According to a usage, which went back to the 17th century, the German bishops were accustomed every five years to request at Rome the faculty of granting certain dispensations (*facultates quinquennales*). The conference of Ems decided that they should thenceforth do without the Papal authorization. The contest lasted a long time, but in the end Rome prevailed. The Bishop of Spires allowed himself to be gained to her cause; the Prince-Bishop of Mayence was accused of aiming at making himself Primate of Germany; the Archbishop of Treves withdrew from the contest; lastly, the Nuncio at Vienna, Caprara, more fortunate than Pacca, who had not been able to induce the king of Prussia, a Protestant, to act against the rebel prelates (*n*), worked so successfully on the mind of Joseph II. that he abandoned a

(*m*) O. Mejer, *Zur Geschichte der römisch-deutschen Frage*, Vol. I. pp. 88 et seq.; Laurent, *Van Espen, Etude historique.*

(*n*) Pacca, *Memorie storiche sul di lui soggiorno in Germania dall' anno* 1786 *al* 1791, *in qualita di nuncio apostolico al Tratto del Reno, dimorante in Colonia*, Modena, 1836.

movement which he had at first embraced with ardour. It is true that in the *Electoral Capitulation*, which was presented to Leopold II. the 30th September, 1790, the Archbishops, Treves excepted, passed an article touching the abolition of the jurisdiction of the Nunciature in the Empire. But that was all. The Nunciature of Cologne, however, soon fell; its 34th and last titulary, Annibale della Genga, afterwards Pope under the name of Leo XII., could not reach his post in 1794 in consequence of the occupation of the town by the French; and the Papacy vainly tried in 1800, 1816 and 1850 to replace, by the establishment of a Nunciature at Berlin, the advanced post it had lost (*o*).

The action of the Nunciature of Vienna is written in characters of blood in the history of Austria, Germany and Hungary. During the Thirty Years' War the representatives of Rome did not cease to inflame the fanaticism of the Emperors, and they have exercised a most deplorable influence on the Austrian monarchy, from that time until a few years ago. There, as elsewhere, they made use of the religious orders, and especially the Jesuits, to gain their ends. Ladislas di Aquino, Nuncio at Lucerne, as we have seen, and having part of Germany within his district, declared that "the Jesuits are the most solid supports which hold poor Germany upright." This was also the opinion of other Nuncios and Popes. But Gregory XV., who knew the Jesuits from having been their scholar, exhorted his Nuncio at Vienna, Caraffa, to deal prudently with them (*p*).

In the Low Countries, the Nunciature of Brussels became the ally of the Jesuits, and laboured to destroy the last traces of independence in the little Catholic Church of Holland; and, as to the Belgian provinces, Joseph II. found himself obliged, in 1787, to expel from Brussels the Nuncio Zondandari.

(*o*) Jacobi, Professor at Halle, *Der Päbstliche Nuntius in Berlin, Eine Streitschrift;* O. Mejer, *Die Propaganda*, Vol. II. pp. 517 et seq.

(*p*) Ranke, *The Popes of Rome*, Vol. III. p. 168.

The Nunciature of Warsaw did not cease to conspire against the peace and repose of Poland.

In Switzerland, the envoy at Lucerne was equally careful to lose no opportunity of sowing discord and hatred among the Cantons. It was the Nuncio Santorio who was the promoter of the Golden Alliance, or Borromean League, sworn 5th October, 1586, between the delegates of Lucerne, Uri, Schwytz, Unterwalden, Zug, Friburg and Solothurn, by which the Catholic Cantons devoted "themselves and their children" to the Holy See. It was he also who urged the same Cantons, excepting Solothurn, to conclude with Phillip II., 12th May, 1587, a convention by which they allowed the passage of the Spanish troops, and received from the king an assurance that he would help them in his turn in the war of religion. Another Nuncio, Ludovico di Conto di Sarego, was the instigator of the massacre of the Reformed of the Valtelina. "It is time," he wrote, "to make Sicilian Vespers of the Lutheran preachers." Everything happened as he wished: one fine day the Reformed were attacked and massacred. The instructions given to the Nuncio Maldeschi deserve consideration. We read there: "Spies are indeed necessary to all Nuncios, but especially so to the Nuncio in Switzerland, because he must spy out the political and ecclesiastical proceedings of the Catholics and of the heretics, on which account your Right Reverence must not fail to have a good spy, who will count the costs for all."

Geneva inspired Rome with real terror. Therefore Rome did not cease to excite France and the Catholic Cantons against her enemy. Gregory XV. distinguished himself in this work. He charged the Nuncio to point out to the Duke of Savoy and the King of France the republican tendencies of the city of Calvin, and to urge them on to war. The independence of bishops was equally an object of the undertakings of the representatives of the Church. At the beginning of the eighteenth century, the Nuncio Caraccioli wished to bring the Swiss Church to a closer obedience. The Bishop of Constance resisted, and protested at Rome. But the Nuncio intrigued so well that he provoked at once a civil and a religious war, the proof of which is that Lucerne itself demanded his recall, "because," said the request, "he has excited to fanaticism and brought on great evils."

These facts allow us to judge of the work of the Nunciatures. We have only cited a few, we could cite yet others, and there is much which it has never been possible to prove. "Die Propaganda ist ein Institut, das nicht von sich spricht," said one day Father Theiner, in speaking of the Congregation of the Propaganda. The Nuncios have acted like the institution on which they depend. Their work has generally been secret, their manœuvres have been subterranean. The evil they have worked has not been the less real.

The occupation of Rome in 1798, the contests between Napoleon and Pius VII., the captivity of Pius VII., and the incorporation of the Pontifical States with the Empire, show what the Papacy had become at the beginning of the century. The negociations of the Concordat of 1801 could not even be invoked in its favour. In international law the Holy See was almost as if it had not existed.

The events of 1815 came to give it some lustre. The Treaties of Vienna re-established the temporal sovereignty of the Popes, and made its spiritual authority shine with a new splendour. The Congress of Vienna adopted, 19th March, 1815, a general regulation concerning the rank of the diplomatic agents, which the Congress which met at Aix-la-Chapelle in 1818, completed. Thenceforward, the ambassadors, the legates, or the Nuncios alone possessed the representative character. No innovation was introduced relative to the representatives of the Pope, while it was arranged that the diplomatic envoys should take rank among themselves, in each class, according to the date of the official notification of their arrival. The Internuncios, ministers of the Pope of the second class, have no right to precedence over their colleagues. In 1849, the Internuncio of the Holy See at the Hague claimed it over the senior of the envoys, Sir Edward

Cromwell Disbrowe, who refused to yield it. Lord Palmerston approved of the action of his agent, relying for proof on the fact that the precedence sanctioned by the regulation of Vienna applied only to Nuncios, that exceptions could not be extended, and that the exception only confirms the previous *status quo* (*q*).

At the Congress, Consalvi ventured to set up the highest pretensions. He desired the re-establishment of the Holy Roman Empire as the centre of Christian unity, the restoration of the Ecclesiastical Principalities, the restitution of all the goods and revenues of the Church, and the re-establishment of the Church in all the rights she held of God and the Apostles. He solemnly protested in the name of Pius VII., 14th June, 1815, "adversus ea quæ in Congressu principum Vindobonensi in præjudicium seu Ecclesiarum Germanicarum sive ipsius S. Sedis Apostolicæ constituto haberentur" (*r*). This was going very far, however violent might have been the reaction against the order of things which had resulted from the revolutionary storm. It is even certain that the restoration of the Patrimony of St. Peter would not have been made on so great a scale had it not been for Bonaparte's escape from the island of Elba, and his re-establishment on the throne. Austria wished to keep the Legations as compensation for the loss of the kingdom of Naples; but the fear of the Hundred Days finished what the jealousy of the other powers and the talent of Consalvi had begun, and the States of the Church were re-constituted.

IV.

In 1815 the Papacy entered on a new era. The Holy Alliance had introduced into the world its illiberal policy.

(*q*) Calvo, *Droit International*, Vol. I. pp. 561 et seq. The Church of Rome generally chuses Cardinals as Legates *à latere*. The Nuncios and Internuncios are prelates of high rank;—the Nuncios are generally Archbishops *in partibus*. A Nuncio who, after his elevation to the cardinalate, continues his functions, is called Pronuncio.

(*r*) The protest of Consalvi is to be found in the *Monumenta Catholica pro independentia potestatis ecclesiasticæ ab imperio civili*, by Roscovany.

So the Curia thought the moment opportune for resuming an international situation. The popes of the 18th century had been in general moderate men; many were even totally devoid of energy. Those of the 19th century will be active and intolerant.

The first act of Pius VII. is characteristic. It was the restoration of the order of Jesuits. The Curia soon tried to re-establish diplomatic relations with the different countries, and to conclude Concordats almost everywhere. The Concordat of 1801 respected Gallican liberties too much for its taste; and it undertook, in 1817, to wring from the Bourbons a more favourable treaty. The negotiations lasted until 1822, but ended in a check. Rome was more fortunate in Germany, and obtained recognition for her bulls of *circumscription* reorganizing the Catholic hierarchy, and put them in force. It must, however, be observed, as Sir Robert Phillimore very well remarks, that "the Papal See had entered into no convention, strictly speaking, with any Non-Roman-Catholic State." On the one part, there were bulls; on the other part, a recognition of these bulls. The bull *De Salute* for Prussia appeared in 1821, and the bull *Imperio Romanorum Pontificum* regulated soon after the situation of Hanover. The negotiations with the Rhenish States at first threatened to fail, as these governments retrenched themselves behind the principles of the Concordat of 1448 and the Declaration of Ems; but, in 1827, the Pope issued the bull *Ad Dominici gregis custodiam*, which established the present dioceses of the province of the Upper Rhine. It should be added that in these different diplomatic acts, the lay authority reserved to itself the rights of sovereignty. The *placet* was maintained in Hanover, the oath of the bishops was required in Prussia, and in the other States the civil power could oppose the election of a bishop.

Rome did not enter into any relation either with Denmark, Sweden or Norway. The kings of Denmark refused to receive the Nuncios of the Pope, because he had claimed spiritual authority by calling them his sons (*s*). Rome had no Concordat with Russia; but the bull of circumscription *Ex imposita* of 30th June, 1818, published with the consent of the Emperor, and completed by the brief of 20th February, 1820, regulated the position of the Catholic Church in this country. And, lastly, there exists no arrangement between the Holy See and Greece and Turkey. We must notice, however, that Leo. XII., in 1826, sent Monsignor Bernetti to Moscow to be present at the coronation of Nicholas I., and that Pius IX., in 1848, sent Monsignor Innocenzo Ferrieri to thank Abdul-Medjid, who had sent Chebid-Effendi, his ambassador at Vienna, to compliment the new Pope.

Austria and Spain, until within the last few years, were among the most faithful allies of the Papacy, as is proved by the Concordats concluded between the governments of Vienna and Madrid and the Holy See.

The situation of England is somewhat interesting. The Roman Catholic hierarchy had fallen in the 16th century; its last representative, Watson, Bishop of Lincoln, had died in 1584. In 1589, the Pope had sent an Archpriest to govern the remains of the Catholic flock, and some years later appeared the Vicars Apostolic. All intercourse with Rome was forbidden.

By the 5 Eliz. c. 1, "if any person shall by writing, printing, preaching or teaching, deed or act, advisedly and wittingly hold or stand with, extol, set forth, maintain or defend the authority, jurisdiction or power of the Bishop of Rome, or of his See, heretofore claimed, used or usurped, within this realm, or by any speech, open deed or act, advisedly and wittingly attribute any such manner of jurisdiction, authority or pre-eminence to the said Bishop or See of Rome within this realm, he, his abettors, procurers and councillors, and also their aiders, assistants and comforters, upon purpose and to the intent to set forth further

(*s*) Martens, *Guide diplomatique*, Vol. I. p. 41.

and extol the said usurped power, being thereof lawfully indicted or presented within one year, and convicted or attainted at any time after, shall incur a *præmunire:* and as well justices of assize in their circuits, as justices of the peace in their quarter or open sessions, may inquire thereof as of other offences against the peace, and shall certify every presentment thereof into the King's Bench within forty days, if the term be then open; if not, at the first day of the full term next following the said forty days, on pain of 100*l.*; and the justices of the King's Bench shall hear and determine the same as in other cases of *præmunire.* And for the second offence such person shall be guilty of high treason; but not to work corruption of blood, disherison of heirs or forfeiture of dower: provided that the charitable giving of reasonable alms to any offender, without fraud or covin, shall not be deemed any such abatement, procuring, counselling, aiding or assisting or comforting, as thereby to incur pain or penalty."

At the beginning of our century, Rome conceived great hopes, which were strengthened by the liberal measures which resulted in the Act of 1829 (*t*). From the diplomatic point of view, however, no change took place; the English law, forbidding every English subject to attribute any authority whatever to the Papal See, was still in force. A curious illustration of that fact occurred in the reign of George IV. The Pope Leo XII. sent a letter announcing his accession to the Pontificate to the King, and, through his secretary, to Mr. Canning, then Secretary of State for Foreign Affairs, who consulted the Attorney and Solicitor-General as to whether a reply to these letters would subject him to a *præmunire.* The answer was in the affirmative. "In compliance with your request," answered the law officers of the Crown, Sir Robert Gifford and Sir John Singleton Copley, "we have carefully perused and considered the letters above referred

(*t*) "Act for the Relief of his Majesty's Roman Catholic Subjects," which was passed on the 13th April, 1829 (10 Geo. 4, c. 7).

to, and beg leave to state that by the stat. 5 Eliz. c. 1, s. 2, advisedly and wittingly to attribute, by any speech, open deed or act, any manner of jurisdiction, authority or pre-eminence to the See of Rome, or to any Bishop of the same See within this realm, subjects a party, for the first offence, to the penalties of *præmunire;* and as the Pope, by virtue of his office, claims, as we conceive, authority, jurisdiction and pre-eminence over the whole Christian Church, and certainly over the Catholic Church in this realm; and, as by the letters, his elevation to the supreme Pontificate is in terms announced, which we apprehend would be construed as importing such a claim, we are of opinion that any answer to these letters, which might be interpreted into an implied recognition of such a claim, might be considered as bringing the party, being a subject, writing or advising it, within the operation of the above statute." The two signatures to this letter have caused it to be observed with reason, that it was worthy of remark, that the legislature, by carefully adopting, in the various acts passed since the Reformation, the title of Bishop of Rome, instead of that of Pope, seemed anxiously to avoid any such implied recognition (*u*).

(*u*) Canning himself read this letter in the House of Commons, 6th March, 1827, and related his own impressions. "Now," he said, "I began to consider with myself the penalties upon *præmunire;* and, unlearned as I was, I found upon inquiry, that a man attainted with *præmunire* might be slain by any one. Further, that he was considered to be out of the King's protection, and beyond that of the law for all beneficial purposes. He was unable to bring his action at law, and no one was to succour a person so guilty. According to Hawkins, I believe, there are further penalties connected with suretyship." The Master of the Rolls: "That is not my opinion." Mr. Secretary Canning: "No; it is not the right honourable gentleman, but Burn's *Justice*, which is my present authority. (A laugh.) Such were some of the penalties incident to a *præmunire*, which I, an ignorant and unlettered person, naturally anxious to obtain information on the subject, discovered. It was natural I should look to the penalties; and, looking to things, I resolved not to correspond with his Holiness the Pope. Accordingly, I did not write a single line in reply to the communication. Neither did I advise his Majesty to return any answer. And, although from that day

The government of Queen Victoria abrogated the ancient legislation. It was made permissible to entertain diplomatic relations with the Sovereign of the Roman States. "Provided always, and be it enacted, that it shall not be lawful for her Majesty, her heirs or successors, to receive at the Court of London as ambassador, envoy extraordinary, minister plenipotentiary, or other diplomatic agent, accredited by the *Sovereign of the Roman States*, any person who shall be in Holy Orders in the Church of Rome, or any Jesuit or member of any Religious Order, Community, or Society of the Church of Rome bound by monastic or religious vows" (11 & 12 Vict. c. 108). We know how the Holy See replied to this condescension of the English government, and how, by letters apostolic of 29th September, 1850, the Pope re-established the Roman Catholic hierarchy in England. From the Roman point of view, it was taking possession of the country, and affirming the Pope's rights to it. This act excited in Great Britain long and violent protestations. The title of the bull, the language it used, the mode of publication—all seemed calculated to insult England. The Anglican Church was roused. Two Archbishops and twenty Bishops protested solemnly by their manifesto of 29th March, 1851; more than three thousand addresses, bearing a million of signatures, were sent to the Queen. Legislation was powerless. The recent laws (7 & 8 Vict. c. 102, and 9 & 10 Vict. c. 59) had repealed the statutes of *præmunire*, and the statutes of Elizabeth relative to Roman bulls, and no one thought of re-enacting them. So that Lord John Russell's Act, to prevent the assumption of certain ecclesiastical titles in respect of places in the

to this, I have been precluded from the possibility of offering to his Holiness any explanation of my apparent want of proper attention and politeness, I may now be permitted to hope that in a more legitimate way my motive may reach his Holiness's ears, and without the fear of a *præmunire*."—Hansard, *Parliamentary Debates*, House of Commons, 6th March, 1827.

United Kingdom (14 & 15 Vict. c. 60), was, on the whole, a weapon without power to strike. We ought to say that the Roman Catholics had loudly affirmed their fidelity and their submission to the laws of their country. Their address, bearing 250,000 signatures, declared that, "The dearest of these privileges to which we have thus been admitted by the wisdom of the British legislature, is that of openly professing and practising the religion of our fathers, in communion with the See of Rome. Under its teaching we have ever learnt, as a most sacred lesson, to give to Cæsar the things that are of Cæsar, as we give to God the things that are of God. In whatever, therefore, our Church has at any time done for establishing its regular system of government amongst its members in this island, we beg most fervently and most sincerely to assure your Majesty that the organization granted to us is entirely ecclesiastical, and its authority purely spiritual. But it leaves untouched every tittle of your Majesty's rights, authority, power, jurisdiction and prerogative, as our sovereign, and as sovereign over these realms; and does not in the leastwise diminish or impair our profound reverence, our loyalty, fidelity, and attachment to your Majesty's august person and throne; and we humbly assure your Majesty, that among your Majesty's subjects there exists no class who more solemnly, more continually, or more fervently pray for the stability of your Majesty's throne, for the preservation of your Majesty's life, and for the prosperity of your Majesty's Empire, in whose religion loyalty is a sacred duty and obedience a Christian virtue" (*x*).

We have not here to enumerate all the diplomatic acts which took place in the 19th century between the Papacy and the different States. Those which we have passed in

(*x*) Sir Robert Phillimore, *International Law*, Vol. II.; Sir Travers Twiss, *The Letters Apostolic of Pope Pius IX. considered with reference to the Law of England and the Law of Europe.*

review are sufficient to show what was, until 1870, the international situation of the sovereign pontiffs considered as heads of the Church. Still less have we to occupy ourselves with the Ultramontane movement which at the present moment carries away Catholicism, and alienates it from the modern world. The insensate declarations of the Encyclicals and of the Syllabus, the proclamation of Papal Infallibility by the Vatican Council, are present to the memory of all, and it only remains that we should examine what answer should be made to the question we proposed at the beginning of our work.

The edifice of the temporal power has fallen amid the applause of the civilized world, and the Papacy now has only a purely spiritual character. History has enabled us to see what position the Holy See attained to in the past when regarded as the supreme authority of the Catholic Church; it has shown us the pretensions of the Roman pontiffs, the reception they met with, and the use which the popes themselves have made of the rights which have been yielded to them. What should be done in our days?

In the Middle Ages the Roman Catholic Church regarded herself as the highest international authority. The law of modern nations rests, on the contrary, not on the authority of religion, or of the Church, but on a politico-social authority—that of humanity and of the States. Is it possible to recognize an authority in Churches, and to consider treaties made between these and the State nearly the same as treaties between State and State? From a theoretical point of view the answer is affirmative. Is it possible to recognize that which personifies these Churches, the positive and actual right of embassy? From a theoretical point of view the answer is still affirmative.

This is the case especially when the Church is not national, that is to say, restricted to the territory of a certain State, but when she has for her distinctive character a universal organization (*y*). This authority and this right will be of a special nature, and the personality thus admitted will be a personality *sui generis*. The Roman Catholic Church, without doubt, does not answer to the aspirations of the modern world, and the historical development of the last centuries tends to free humanity from her tutelage. There is not a State which has not had on this account to enter into struggles, which have been sometimes terrible; there is not one which can, under pain of perishing, abandon the field of battle. The Papacy has placed itself in opposition to the march of civilization, and it has been necessary to treat it as an adversary and an enemy. Would there not be imprudence in reinvesting it now with any sovereignty whatever? Here is found all the difficulty. Nothing in pure theory makes it necessary to acknowledge that the Holy See has any international rights. Is it advantageous to grant benevolently privileges which it is allowable to refuse it?

The question is, above all, a question of fact, the solution of which may differ in various States and countries. Logic is a bad counsellor in politics, and it is necessary to guard against being carried away by passion. Where the separation of Church and State is not part of the fundamental laws of the country, it may be useful to maintain relations with the Holy See, just as it may be useful to end them. No Government has a juridical obligation to maintain a diplomatic post for the Papacy, but it may have a considerable interest in observing such a line of conduct. To keep the Papacy outside of international law, to ignore it, to leave it in consequence a free field, and to allow it to lead in its own manner the Ultramontane movement which is breaking loose all over the world,—to permit all this might lead to far more inconvenience and much greater dangers than the international recognition of the Holy See and the maintenance of diplomatic relations with it

(*y*) Bluntschli, *Das moderne Völkerrecht*, Book II. art. 26.

could present. The Italian law of guaranties of 13th May, 1871, has proclaimed in this respect ideas which seem to us just (z).

There is yet another argument to bring forward. In a despatch addressed by Lord Palmerston, 5th January, 1849, to the Marquis of Normanby, ambassador at Paris, the English Minister of Foreign Affairs emphatically said, "that no doubt it was obviously desirable that a person who in his spiritual capacity has great and extensive influence over the internal affairs of most of the countries of Europe should be in such a position of independence as not to be liable to be used by any one power as a political instrument for the annoyance of any other power." On this account Lord Palmerston believed that it would be well that the Pope should be sovereign of a sufficient territory. The idea of restoring the States of the Church to the Pope must be given up. The unity of Italy is an accomplished fact; it is a fortunate fact, and one which all the partisans of progress have applauded and always will applaud. But the fundamental idea of the English despatch does not the less remain unshaken. There would be danger in allowing the Papacy, the supreme authority of the most numerous of the Christian Churches, to fall into a state of tutelage under a single government, and become a mere instrument in the hands of Italy.

We have spoken of the law of guaranties which assures to the Papacy an exceptional situation. Its first article declares the person of the Pope *sacra ed inviolabile*. Art. 3 declares that the Italian Government "rende al sommo Pontifice nel territorio del Regno gli onori sovrani." It maintains "le preminenze d' onore riconosciutegli dai Sovrani Catolici." Before this law was made the Italian Minister of Foreign Affairs had sent, on 18th October,

(z) See on the subject of the Italian law of guaranties the *Diritto diplomatico* of Pietro Esperson, Professor at the University of Pavia, Nos. 51, etc.; and the essay of Von Holtzendorff, *Völkerrechtliche Erläuterungen zum italienischen Garantiegesetz*.

1870, a circular dated from Florence and addressed to the Italian diplomatic representatives abroad. He solemnly declared in this document the firm intention of Italy to respect the independence of the Holy See. "The lofty position which personally belongs to the Holy See shall in no degree be lowered. Its sovereign character, its pre-eminence over the other Catholic princes, the immunities and the civil list which belong to it in this character, shall be amply guaranteed, its palaces and residences shall have the privilege of exterritoriality. The exercise of its high spiritual mission shall be secured to it by a double order of guaranties, by free and incessant communication with the faithful, by the Nunciatures to the powers which it shall continue to have, by the representatives which the powers will continue to accredit; and lastly, and above all, by the separation of the Church and the State which Italy has already proclaimed, and which the King's Government proposes to apply in his territory as soon as Parliament shall have sanctioned the projects of the counsellors of the Crown." This language is perfect. The law of guaranties, which is its consecration, gives satisfaction politically and legally. But if the various governments should wish to continue to maintain the Papacy in the rank it occupies outside of Italy, if they wish to expect that the Pope shall not be subject in everything to the will of the Italian Government, it is necessary that they should have representatives at his court, and that they should in turn admit his representatives.

There is, besides, a consideration which ought to be taken into account. The dangers presented by the institution of Nuncios and their double character, political and religious, are, without doubt, only too serious. We have seen the Nunciatures at work in these last centuries, and we have been able to prove clearly what perils they presented to the independence of Church and State. But the proclamation of Infallibility and the centralizing movement of the last few years have placed Catholicism in such a position that the system of National Churches may be considered as vanquished for ever. The evil in this direction is done and is irreparable; whatever precautionary measures modern States may adopt with regard to the Nuncios, they will not succeed in remedying it. If the sole desire of protecting its clergy and bishops induces a country to break off diplomatically with the Holy See, it will lose its labour, and Rome will know how to find other representatives than its ordinary Nuncios. It is at Rome itself that the governments, taking advantage of the centralization of Catholicism, ought to operate; instead of confining themselves to defend on their own territory their rights of sovereignty, they ought to try to lead the Papacy to ideas which would be less in contradiction with the spirit of progress and of liberty; and from this point of view a representation of the great powers at the See of Rome may be of great utility.

The ideas expressed by Prince Bismarck relative to the displomatic position of the Holy See deserve to be thought over. This illustrious statesman has occupied himself with the subject at different times. In 1872, on the eve of the confessional struggle, he declared to the Prussian Chamber of Deputies that three or four years before he had called the attention of the King to the question of the expediency of establishing a Nunciature at Berlin. On the 14th May of the same year, he said in the Diet that he regretted that the Court of Rome had refused shortly before to consent to the choice made by Germany of a Cardinal, the Prince of Hohenlohe, as representative of the Empire to the Holy See, and he added that he did not think it the less necessary to maintain the post of the Vatican in the hope of a future understanding with Rome. The year following, when the discussion on the budget of foreign affairs took place in the Reichstag, a deputy proposed to cancel the sums inscribed in the budget for diplomatic representation to the Holy See. The Chancellor again combatted the motion, and the article was voted. But in

1874 the title relating to the post of envoy to the Holy See was withdrawn before the public discussion, and at the session of the Reichstag of 5th December, Prince Bismarck made a most remarkable speech explaining the views of the government. While admitting that the character of head of a religious confession which has adherents in Germany is not by itself a reason why the Empire should send him a diplomatic representative, he laid great stress on the motive of the line of conduct adopted, namely, the claims set up by the Papacy,—claims incompatible with all regular political government. In his opinion, until the question of the Roman claims was decided, the Empire of Germany could not recognize a power which encouraged a part of the German population to resist the laws of the country, nor yet could give cause for belief that any such recognition would be granted. But in the sitting of the Prussian Chamber of Deputies, 16th April, 1875, he did not conceal that he hoped that one day, that soon, as he said, a pacific Pope would occupy the Holy See, and that then a minister of the Pope would be found sufficiently wise to seek to make peace with the secular power (*a*).

In his treatise on the *Responsibility and Irresponsibility of the Pope in International Law*, Bluntschli has suggested an idea which perhaps may be practically realized, and which approaches the ideas of Prince Bismarck. In order to prevent usurpations and hostile political acts on the part of the Popes, he inquires whether the States cannot, in conceding the juridical privilege of the Papacy, require that the Popes should respect the legal and constitutional order of the countries granting it, and should not exercise against the States any act prohibited by international law. If this were so, the religious peace of the world would be assured, Catholicism would follow the example given it by

(*a*) *Discours du Prince de Bismarck*, Vol. VI. pp. 54, 99.

other Christian Churches, and certainly we should never see renewed the spectacle afforded by Pius IX. when, in quite modern times, he quashed the laws of great countries like Austria and Prussia.

This eminent writer goes yet further. According to him, an International Convention of all Christian States, or at least of the principal, could regulate the conditions and terms of the international privileges of the Papacy. The Convention might be presented to the Popes on their election, as the Electoral Capitulation formerly was to the Emperors, and the recognition by the States of the Pope, as Head of the Church, would depend on the Pope's promise. This proposal seems less practical than the first. The fact that the Governments were uninterested in the nomination of the present Pope does not surely forebode their thinking of acting in concert to regulate his status. The isolated action of the different countries is preferable. Besides, there are States which would never interfere in religious affairs, and it is necessary to leave them their freedom.

We have been speaking of States in which the Church and the Civil Power are not completely separated. What must be said of those in which the neutrality of the Government in religious affairs is absolute?

Can these States allow Rome any authority whatever? The question does not seem to us for a moment doubtful. Being an authority purely spiritual, the Holy See is to these governments as though it did not exist, and the State cannot, without forsaking its own sphere, and trampling under foot the essential principles of its constitution, entertain diplomatic relations with it. The absolute separation of Church and State may be attacked and censured: it is allowable to denounce it as an illogical and dangerous principle; but as soon as it is admitted, it is necessary to admit its consequences also, and one of these consequences is, that all relations with such a spiritual institution as the Papacy of our days should be carefully avoided.

There is another case which may occur, and which, in fact, has already occurred. Can a government, not maintaining a diplomatic representative at the Holy See, admit the presence of a Nuncio accredited to itself? It evidently can. A State which has a right to receive ministers, is not thereby, unless it has bound itself by treaties, under obligation to maintain diplomatic representatives. The conduct of Holland, which admits an Internuncio at the Hague, but has withdrawn its minister from Rome, is in no way contrary to the principles and practice of international law (*b*).

V.

When the history of the relations between the Papacy and Civil Governments is passed in review, one phenomenon especially strikes the mind; almost always the Papacy has assumed an attitude hostile to progress and liberty. In the Middle Ages, at the time of the Reformation, and still in our days, the Holy See represents tendencies contrary to the tendencies of humanity. This fact cannot be too much regretted. The Catholic Church, a daughter of Christianity, might have been able, as the Protestant Churches were afterwards, to labour for the moral advancement of the world, and for the advent of the reign of liberty on the earth. But she has failed in her mission. Is a Reform of Catholicism still possible? It will be admitted without difficulty that much will depend on the solution of this question which the future will give. The religious sentiment exists in humanity—it has its imperious exigencies, and history shows us of how much importance it is to satisfy them rationally. On the other hand, the appearance of a new religion may be considered in our time as an impossibility, and it may be affirmed with equal

(*b*) Martens, *Guide diplomatique*, Vol. I. p. 40.

reason that the passage of an entire people from one religion to another will not take place. There is, therefore, very great interest in knowing if the Roman Catholic Church may not yet reverse the separation she has pronounced between her own doctrines and modern ideas.

At first sight, we perceive that distinguished minds have answered the questions in the negative. In reality the actual direction of Christianity is altogether within the hands of the partisans of ultramontanism, who have managed so as to make any movement of renovation as difficult as can be imagined. Pius IX. had become an instrument of their will. Nothing as yet proves that Leo XIII. has shaken off a crushing tutelage. The bishops no longer have either personal authority or personal power; the clergy is brought up in the most exalted principles, and the modern constitution of the Church allows no influence to the lay element. More than that, the fundamental points of Ultramontane doctrines have been proclaimed dogmas of faith, and thus it is that they can no longer be attacked without laying a sacrilegious hand on the religious edifice.

Besides, it is very necessary to observe that the various attempts which have succeeded each other during the last sixty years for the purpose of starting Catholicism on a progressive course, have ended in results of a nature to cause those to hesitate who would give an affirmative answer to the problem we are examining. Even before the Vatican Council had proclaimed the rupture of Catholicism with modern ideas,—even before the Popes had published their Encyclicals and their Syllabus,—Wessenberg failed in his attempt to constitute a National Church, and, later still, new efforts have in Germany been equally unfortunate failures. Do we not see since 1870 that the Old Catholics make but few proselytes? And yet this movement arose from most favourable circumstances. How then can we admit that a revolution in the Roman Church has any chances of success?

Notwithstanding the actual triumph of ultramontanism,

—notwithstanding the repeated checks of the Catholic renovators,—we are yet led to believe, that in a future, more or less distant, a movement of reform may be produced in the Roman Church. Can any one question, that there are in that Church a multitude of minds who are offended by her religious despotism,—that in the ranks of the clergy, and even of the episcopate, there are priests who desire nothing better than to free themselves from the Ultramontane yoke, as recent manifestations have proved? In Austria, in Hungary, in Bavaria, in America, in yet other countries, there are bishops who see with grief the Catholic Church, which they love and venerate, engage herself in a road from which there is no issue. Even in the Council of the Vatican, it must not be forgotten, out of 601 voters, there was a minority of eighty-eight members, and sixty-two members declared that they admitted the new dogma only conditionally. And the greater part of these prelates occupied the most important Episcopal Sees. There exists therefore certainly a moderate liberal fraction in the Roman Catholic religion, and this fraction contains elements important enough to claim to govern the Church.

Renovating movements have hitherto failed, and the complete centralization of the Church constitutes a huge obstacle to those which may yet take place. Lord Palmerston said one day in speaking of European governments, that the first which would think of troubling the general peace would see the whole of Europe unite to crush it. This saying is perfectly applicable to Catholicism. The priest or the bishop who will raise the standard of revolt will have against him the entire ecclesiastical hierarchy. But centralization itself is as much a source of weakness as of strength to Ultramontanism. If the head of the Church, if the infallible Pope should not completely hold the excessive ideas of the Jesuits,—if he should wish to be, and should be in reality more than an instrument in their hands,—what would then become of the system so laboriously built up by the chiefs of the Ultramontane party? Now, is it abusing hypothesis too much to admit the possibility of a wise and enlightened sovereign Pontiff? Is a liberal Pope in reality, as an eminent writer has said, *the most impossible of impossibilities?* Does not history show us, in the past century, a man of large and tolerant ideas seated in St. Peter's chair. We will not venture to pronounce an opinion. The future has its secrets, which it is useless to seek to penetrate. But the modern State may reserve to itself an important part to play in the solution of the problem of the reconciliation of freedom and of Catholicism, and it is in this respect that the recognition of the international personality of the Holy See can offer incontestable advantages.

In his remarkable work *on Politics*, the result of long study, and of many years in the practice of governing, Bluntschli says that the modern State should take charge of the education of the Ultramontanes (*c*). Still, under the influence of the doctrines of the Middle Ages, they see in the State only a material and terrestrial kingdom, which they esteem very lightly when they compare it to the Church in which they bow to the spiritual and eternal kingdom of God. They require, therefore, that a severe and rigorous discipline should form their minds, and make them really perceive the sovereignty, the wisdom, the creative power of the State, and show them the superiority of the manly spirit which animates the State. No one will contest the justice of these ideas. And what then prevents their being applied to a larger sphere, where it is no longer a mere fraction of a certain notion which is in question, but an important part of humanity?

There is here an important argument in favour of the maintenance of diplomatic relations between the Government and the Court of the Vatican. In the present constitution of the Catholic Church the Papacy will always know how to exert its influence on the faithful; it will

(*c*) Bluntschli, *Die Politik als Wissenschaft*, pp. 497 et seq.

always know, whether a State acknowledges its juridical personality or not, how to lead, according to its wish, the episcopate and the clergy of that State. Why not then derive from such a situation all the advantage possible? The Papal privilege would imply for the Papacy duties from the fulfilling of which it could not escape with impunity. On the other hand, the different governments would know, perhaps, how to prevent the Holy See from excess. Now, this is a most essential point. It is not in the power of any one to say whether the efforts that might be made would succeed. But if it cannot be affirmed, it would be daring to deny it, and in any case, one trial would not be too much. On the day when this last experiment shall fail, and when a divorce shall be irremediably pronounced between Catholicism and civilization, a radical solution will be necessary, but then the Popes must take on themselves the evil they have wrought to their Church and to Religion.

Made in the USA
Monee, IL
04 November 2026

67388656R10046